Acknowledgements

Thank you for the continued support. Through thick and thin you have inspired me to be a better person; now I show the world how you helped me.

A Bit About the Author

The author does not matter; the only important person in this book is you.

Copyright

http://www.thesecretsofforgiveness.com/

Table of Contents

Introduction – I Sin. Please Forgive Me

I fuck, I lie and I cheat. All the sins a man can commit I have committed. Is there any point of even trying to redeem myself?

Are you for real? This has plagued humankind with guilt for centuries.

Yes it has, and you sit by and allow us to punish ourselves, day in day out.

Okay so I'll simplify it for you. Why would the Almighty creator allow humankind to "sin" if I never wanted them? Yes, there are flaws in your design, but this is not one of them. Of all the things that humankind has done this dumbfounds me the most. Why do you carry on punishing yourself for so-called "sin"? What does "sin" even mean?

You're asking me what sin means? You're supposed to be the Almighty lol.

Yes I am, I am asking you what you think sin is.

Sin is doing all the things we dream of doing, but we are too scared of doing because we don't want to go to hell.

Yes, if you "sin" you will end up in hell, so I give you the option of free will to do what you want to do, and then slap you for doing it.

Was that sarcasm?

Yes it was. I am the creator of light and the bringer of love. Does punishing you for free will sound loving to you? Let's just rearrange how you think about sin. At the time of the sin you enjoy the sin, then you feel guilty about the sin and then you go to hell and burn and play with Hitler. Accept that Hitler went to heaven.

Heaven? Are you for real? I am so getting killed for this book.

Please don't kill the messenger, he is just a vessel. Humankind has a habit of killing my messengers. Not that you ever succeeded in killing them in the first place.

What do you mean? They never died?

I'll explain later, but first let me get back to sin. So you "sin", then you cry about "sinning", and then punish yourself for "sinning", and then so-called loved ones remind you every day of the "sin".

Yep, I get reminded every day of the sins that I have done, lucky for me the people around me don't know all of them.

Son, you can handle others reminding you of your "sins", but how much do you punish yourself?

It's normal to punish yourself, it's what us men do.

It's not just men that punish themselves for "sins", it's all of humankind. So now that you

understand that there is no such thing as "sin", let's move onto the next issue humankind has.

What are you on about? Not enough content and you're making no sense?

Yes I am making sense, and the content is spot on. If humankind cannot understand my message in this book, then humankind is not ready for enlightenment and unconditional love.

Let me simply say it for the readers. I shall not sin - as I can't sin since there is no such thing.

Stop making it up as you go along. I'll simplify it for you: I give you free will to do whatever you want to do, so why would I punish you for using your free will?

That kind of makes sense, but not enough content.

Just go with it for now. Let's move on to your next worry, "I shall not kill". The spirit and soul never die, humankind has proven this time after time - your so-called science has proven this. Why does everything in the world have to make sense?

Well if it doesn't make sense, how does it work?

Everything does not need to make sense. Just accept that humankind still lacks knowledge, and accept that a greater power is at work.

Well you're going to say that.

Okay, let me stop you there. Here is me, the Almighty creator, giving you this beautiful message, and you are more worried about getting to work. Really, is this what humankind has come to? Keep your notepad and pen close to your heart and I'll be back.

Chapter 1- The Sin of Love, Sorry I Mean Sex, Please Forgive Me

The two strongest emotions I have given you are love and hate. Why does humankind confuse lust and love? They substitute wealth for love just to have an "easy life". I have created the world, which has an abundance of everything. It is your birthright to love, have good health and true wealth in abundance. Everyone is born happy, full of love and a millionaire, but you stop your own birthright.

I understand what you are on about, but some of the novice readers might struggle.

If they are struggling they can Google it.

Shall I just fill in the blanks?

Every time I have left humankind to fill in the blanks a new religion is born.

Getting off topic?

You as a messenger were born off-topic.

Is this you telling me I am a mistake?

There is no such thing as a mistake, but I'll break it down for you.

Everyone is born a millionaire - it is your God-given right to have an abundance of everything, including health, money and love.

Yes, you may interrupt me like a child.

At the age of thirty-one, I don't see myself as a child but let's go with it.

Just ask your question.

What about children born into poor health, abusive families etc, how can they be born with an abundance of health?

Normally there are two takes on this: the first one is that you choose your parents, so therefore it is lessons you needed to learn. The Almighty creator does not punish. The second take is you are paying for the sins of your last lifetime - please read the introduction, "I shall not sin".

Okay, I am still confused.

So remember when I said humanity had two flows? Well this is one of them. When a child is conceived, at that moment, the child has abundance and a god-given right of abundance. As soon as it is conceived the child is born in my eyes, and not at what humankind calls birth.

So how does that answer the question of abuse or children born out of ill health?

I will re-state what I have just told you: when a child is conceived it has an abundance of health,

wealth etc. But it is then the parents' responsibility to keep it that way.

I can't agree with what you are saying. So you're telling me every child is "born" healthy, but the parents affect the child?

Yes, and the reason why you don't agree is because you are not the creator. I am.

A bit arrogant this morning?

No, not at all. You are just the messenger, and a lot of what you are writing you will not understand or agree with. Just do your job.

That was harsh, lol.

At least you saw the funny side. Most would just cry. Let's get back on topic. Accept that every action has a consequence, the universe as you know it is made of energy, and the energy never dies - it just changes shape or form. So every thought is important. Whether positive or negative, it affects the universe. I can tell you're getting very frustrated with what I am saying.

Yes, I am, I think you are full of shit and don't want to take responsibility for your failings.

Why are you angry?

So much going on, so much pain and hurt. If you showed yourself just once, humankind would become better.

Is that what you really think? Yes, I have the power to stop the so-called "wrongs" of the world. Remember the introduction: no such thing as right or wrong. But the greatest gift I gave humankind was free will, so after billions of years, yes billions of years, why would I change it now? I show myself to the world in different forms every day, from the book you read to the song you hear to the article you read on your phone.

We are getting off topic. Do you think we have covered an abundance of health to your satisfaction?

No, we have not.

Then, my son, you are not ready to understand my teachings. So let's just move onto the next topic: abusive parents.

There is no such thing as bad or good parents, as there is no sin. So in your eyes abusive parents are bad, but they act out of free will.

You are really struggling with this topic.

Yes, I am. So you're saying a three-month-old baby has an abundance of love even if its parents rape the baby? Yes, there are sick people out there.

Love does not just come from other humans; the universe is the true bringer of pure love. You are surrounded by love, but humankind has not evolved enough to see or understand that. Let me give you some examples:

The sunlight that hits your eyes when waking up is pure love.

The feel of your blanket on your skin.

The feel of rain or the cold on your lips is pure love.

The sound of birds singing in the morning is pure love.

I gave humankind six senses to feel the love of the universe. You are so frustrated with this topic, but you, my son, should understand it better than most. You have developed your sixth sense and feel the love of the universe directly.

I do understand the loving aspect of the universe a bit better. We are coming to the end of the chapter and we still have not mentioned my favourite subject, sex.

I love your sense of humour.

I thought you were only doom and gloom, love your neighbour and shit?

I created humour, and no I'm not going to tell you a joke, this is not play time.

Okay, can I add my own joke?

No.

Can we talk about sex, please?

You sound like a sex pest.

Was that a joke?

No.

Really? Kick a man while he's down?

Would I ever do that? Let's get back to the topic as your hand is hurting from writing and you will cry like a little girl later on.

Sex is the ultimate connection humans can have with one another. It heightens most of your experiences such as love, lust, hate and desire. Just ask the question!

What are your views on gay sex?

If I never wanted gay sex, would I allow it?

Does that mean you support gay sex?

I support one thing and one thing only: free will. Ask yourself, would I allow man on man sex or woman on woman sex if I did not want it? Not only did I want this as an option, I made sure humankind could enjoy it regardless of which they chose. Speak to a bisexual person and ask them which they prefer, and they will most likely tell you the person they loved the most rather than being gender specific.

You have a twisted mind.

Thought you were not judgemental. I think I am just being curious.

Ask the question.

What about humans that have sex with animals (at no point have I ever considered this, but we all know someone that has watched animal farm).

The last sentence did make me laugh. Again, there is no right or wrong. Humankind has free will. Ask the question.

Would you fuck an animal?

(Shakes in disbelief.) I am the creator of all, the father and mother of all. I have never had sexual contact with any of my creations.

So you're a virgin?

In your human eyes yes, but I do not lack companionship.

Is there a Mr. and Mrs. Creator?

There is no point having this conversation as humankind would not understand. You don't even have the words in your vocabulary.

So sex is not good or bad, but just a method to heighten emotions?

Yes, and to reproduce if wanted. I mentioned flaws in humankind's design. One of the flaws is

that from the point of conception to the point of "birth" a lot can change.

What other flaws do we have?

Humankind applies logic to everything. Accept some things don't work within the laws of logic and see the universe the way I do.

Chapter 2 – The Price of Forgiveness

Look how excited you get when you read the title, because you have to pay a price. Look around you and all the wonders that are free in the world: food, water and compassion. But it is poor choices by humankind that limit your experience - you limit your experience.

I never limit my experience, I enjoy every day, I love the wonders of the world.

Who are you trying to lie to, me or yourself? Deep down you know the truth.

Okay, so how do I change it?

The power of the universe is all around you; you just have to accept its teachings and power.

How do you do that?

Easy. Open your mind and soul to love, and love every aspect of your life, even the aspects you "want" to change.

Why is "want" in speech marks?

Humankind has failed for billions of years with its "wants". Ask both questions. I am ready.

How have we been alive for billions of years? And everyone wants something, is that not the reason to pray? To ask for forgiveness, ask for more money or for love etc?

The issue with understanding humanity's age comes from your understanding of time. Time is not dimensional. It is not horizontal or vertical. You do not have the understanding to process time.

There is nothing wrong with praying for wanting more, but the universe will give you exactly what you want.

I get it, humankind is thick, but I don't understand how you said the universe gives it as it is, and you the creator don't.

Thank you for cutting me off mid-sentence. We will come back to the last question. When you pray, you ask, "I want more money," so the universe makes sure you get what you want, "the want for more money". The universe gives you what you ask for.

So all I have to do is say thank you for a billion pounds and bam it's mine?

Yes and no. The first part is saying it, the second part is believing it, the third part is acting upon it, and the fourth part is manifesting it with love. Do all five and it will happen.

Ermmmm you only listed four. What is number five?

That is for humankind to work out.

That's just teasing, feels like foreplay without banging.

I promise you number five by the end of the book.

Can we get back to the topic about the universe and you?

Yes, we can son, in the simplest way I can explain it. I am the creator; I created the universe and all the beings inside it. The universe oversees the running of the universe.

I am so confused right now.

Imagine a wasteland, then I, the creator, visualise and create a school in it that I enjoy creating. Would I then decide to run the school, or employ a head teacher to run it for me? Would a builder be able to do head teacher's job? Yes, they would, but would they be able to it to the same level as an experienced head teacher?

So you created the universe to run itself?

Yes. The universe responds to free will. What you ask for, the universe shall provide.

I with all my heart and love believe I am the creator. Did it work?

Yes, my son, as humankind was created in my image and you create on a daily basis. I, the creator, seek out other creators. A great leader is not "judged" by their leadership but by their ability to create other leaders.

So you the creator are seeking other creators, is this a test?

No, my son, this is not a test, as a test has right or wrong answers, and I believe in free will.

I am totally confused, so it's not a test but you're looking for other creators from humankind? Also, I take it there is more than one creator? Is there a league? And if yes, how are you doing? Lol. So is it a test for you as a creator to see how good you are? And if I was judging you I would say you are shit.

Stop. No I am not shit, and let me answer the questions above. It's difficult for me to explain as your vocabulary and understanding cannot comprehend how big the galaxy is - and no, we don't call it a galaxy. So let me help you picture it. Imagine your galaxy, times that by a billion, then times that by a billion, and that's just one galaxy. Now picture that galaxy, times it by a billion, then times it by another billion. That's how many "galaxies" I have created. Then times it by a billion and then times that by another billion, and that's how many creators there are.

Whohooooo that's a lot of practice and competition.

No, I have not fucked this universe up. If anything it is one of my better creations.

Fuck me, if we are one of your better creations I feel sorry for the "galaxies" that you fucked up. Lol.

You, my son, are just ungrateful. But I do enjoy your sense of humour.

Yes, I am looking for more creators.

Has any of humankind ever aspired to become a creator?

No.

Are we even close?

Give or take a few billion years.

What are the criteria for becoming a creator? I have a killer C.V. and I once created something on Minecraft!

Lol. You are going to have lots of fun writing these books.

Fuck me, did you say books? I am struggling with the first one. What happens if this doesn't even get published?

I guarantee you this will be a multi-million-pound book.

But getting back to topic, as I mentioned, there is more than one creator, no we are not in a league, and no, we do not compete with one another. If anything we help each other. Ask the question.

Can we elect a new creator?

No.

Thought we had free will? And 90% of the ungrateful world would probably elect Steve the creator over you.

You still misunderstand me. I am the creator of the universe, not the caretaker of the universe. The caretaker so to speak is the universe itself. Let's use the school again as an example. Would you blame the builder if the head teacher was doing a bad job?

Well, if the builder employed the head teacher then yes, I would.

So I am to blame for the misfortune of humankind as I created/employed the head teacher, i.e. the universe. Is that what you are trying to communicate?

Let's say if I employed a manager to run my company, who is responsible, the person hiring or the person hired?

It would depend on the thinking of the person answering the question.

Stop side-stepping the question and answer it.

You are trying to find faults where there are none to find, my son. The universe responds to you, not to me the creator. This was the best possible way to make sure free will existed without the creator (me) interfering.

Got to give it to you, a good answer, I am impressed. I was ready for the old one-two.

I created the old one-two.

Lol, even when the questions get tough you glide through. The last question for the day I promise, so if you are so concerned with free will, will this book not affect it?

It will be humankind's choice to act upon what they read here, like everything in life is a choice. As creators we are prepared to nudge you in the right direction.

What direction are you pushing us towards?

To one day become creators like us.

How do we do that?

You already know the answer to that: spiritual enlightenment. And yes, this chapter is done.

Chapter 3 – To Be or Not to Be Spiritual?

Everyone is spiritual, whether they want to accept it or not. You are born, you die and then recycle. You come to learn lessons.

Stop, you said earlier that this is not a test. Now you're saying we are here to learn lessons. Who decides on the lessons we learn? You?

You, my son, decide on the lessons you want to learn. After your physical passing, you return to the realm of spirit (Heaven) where you watch your past life and this life, no judgment, no right or wrong. After analysing it, you decide what lessons you want to learn, and then you ask the universe to manifest them. And let me reconfirm, there is no such thing as hurting anyone as that would mean there is right and wrong.

So let's say in one of my lifetimes I was a paedo, does that mean in the next lifetime I will be abused as a child? One lifetime I physically kill another human being, does that mean I will be murdered in the next one? Because that to me sounds as I am paying for the sins of the last lifetime.

Maybe "lessons" wasn't the best word to use, but it is the closest word you have in your vocabulary.

It's getting old now, all I keep hearing is "you are too stupid to understand", how many times are you going to use this line?

No, you are not stupid. The human vessel has not evolved enough to understand, but the spirit has, so let's call it an appraisal.

Okay, let's go with it. So we as humans appraise ourselves and then decide on what lessons we want to "learn". What are the KPIs (Key Performance Indicators)?

There is one simple KPI, one end result, one single goal: for every spirit in the universe to become a creator.

Now let me stop you there. A billion times a billion: that is the number of lifetimes I predict before any of humankind's spirits become me.

How many lifetimes has the average human spirit had?

15,462 lifetimes. Yes, that figure does not make sense. Accept that this is not the first planet you have had physical life on.

I am really struggling because that seems like a hell of a long time.

Time is not real, but man-made; it was the only way humankind could understand the love of the sun and nature. Instead of just loving everything around itself humankind complicated it with its desire to understand everything.

So every lifetime we learn lessons that help us towards our one true goal to become you, and to become you we have to become more spiritually enlightened?

Yes, you are correct.

Stab in the dark, lol sounds so wrong. Are all the "lessons" we learn spiritually based?

Yes, and now you have answered your own question in regard to a paedophile being the abused in their next lifetime, as there is nothing to gain spiritually from pain, misery, anger etc.

So what lessons do we need to learn to become spiritually more aware? Or spiritually evolved?

Well giving you a blueprint would be counterproductive to the end goal. What is the point of free will if you only want to follow instructions?

Here you go, this is where I need you to get to but I'm not going to tell you how to do it?

Just get on with it?

A bit of trial and error?

Yes, to most of that, but no to the trial and error, as trial and error would indicate right and wrong.

So a bit like Sunday morning football, hope for the best?

Well as a creator I can steer humankind in the right direction. A lot of the time this is

misunderstood, and a new religion is born every time.

So why not just show yourself, fuck free will and help humankind evolve spiritually?

You do make me laugh, and yes I have considered it. But free will stops me. And could you imagine if I actually appeared?

The suicide rate would go through the roof, and humankind would misunderstand me. They would suddenly be full of grief, anger, regret and guilt, all the emotions that I am trying to steer humankind away from. So instead of appearing, as you would say, it is better for me to communicate with humankind through you, and this will better help them in reaching enlightenment.

So from your last comments, suicide is counterproductive to the enlightenment process? How would becoming more spiritual help humankind feel the love?

Suicide limits your human physical experience, but it also has a lasting effect on the people that loved you for years, or even the person that found your body or sees your suicide, so all in all, yes, it is counterproductive, but it does not set you back spiritually.

Could you not say that about death in general, when your loved ones die?

No, as when your loved ones die you have no control over it. Suicide you have direct control

over, and your loved ones replay it over and over again, asking themselves if they could have done something to change the outcome.

You have witnessed the love of the universe first hand: it is time to tell your story and explain how being more spiritual changed your life.

Do I really have to?

Why are you scared to share your story, son? If I do not judge, why do you care about the judgement of others?

It's not the judgement of others that scares me but the judgement of the ones I love.

But no one shall judge, as they who judge are only judging their own lives. And yes, son, I do know it's going to be difficult, but like every story, this story has a very happy ending.

Okay so let start at the age of ten, raped, abused sexually by non-family members as a child, this went on for two years, that's when my childhood ended.

How did you feel?

Different emotions went through me on a regular basis, as a 10-year-old I enjoyed the sexual experience as I never knew any better. Age 12-14 the sexual abuse stopped and it changed to physical and emotional. By the age of 15, I decided to do something about it. I decided to focus on the gym and martial arts. This turned me into a complete animal, the bullied soon became the bully.

I then went to university and my philosophy from a young age was that I had paid for any sins I might commit in this life, as I saw my abuse as a debt for all the evil I was going to do.

Second philosophy, hit first, ask questions later.

Third philosophy, if it breathes, it bangs (women over 18 only).

I found violence funny. Woman had no value in my life apart from family. I was fighting at least twice a week on the streets and the number of women I fucked I can't even remember.

When I was 20, I had my heart broken by my first love and hit rock bottom, suicide letter was done and bam I was ready to commit suicide.

It was a failed attempt, I never had the balls to do it. A consequence of the abuse was that I become a sex addict, different people every day, now reflecting on my actions all I see is a broken me. After my suicide attempt, I was introduced to Louise Hay's How to Heal Your Life and my spiritual journey started.

At 24 I met another love of my life who I married and divorced, lol. Married at 29, divorced by 31. And to be fair to myself, I did keep it in my pants whilst I was married. Turning point in my last marriage, January 2nd, 2015, after six months of hell, I decided on suicide attempt number two, suicide letter written and failed attempt number two. Growing trend of failure lol.

March 2015 psychic/clairvoyant number one. I went with expectations of bullshit, scamming fuckers, easiest way to make money, they were lower in my eyes than the priests and other religious men and woman. But I was surprised, it was okay and it gave me hope, I always knew there was a greater power out there but never believed humankind could make contact with the greater power, how wrong was I?

Mid-March 2015 all I kept meeting/rebounding with was beautiful girls, talk about overachieving. May 2015 introduced clairvoyant/healer number two, Lynn Round, who is now a second mother to me. She was spot on in my reading, what age the abuse started, the type and when and how it happened. I mean stuff I had never told another soul and she knew. That's when I was 100% certain a greater power was out there. She then drew six cards for my love life. One gets dropped/dumped straight away. One out of the six I had not met yet, and the other four I dated over the next few months.

June 2015 I am asked to attend a guided meditation class to make contact with spirits. So even though I believed in Lynn I did not believe in myself. First meditation I had no idea what to expect apart from "I see dead people" (as quoted in films).

Okay, you don't actually see dead people; well I have never done, in a class with another 15 people hoping to make contact with spirits. So we go on a journey that lasts around 20 minutes and on the way out you have a gatekeeper who gives you two presents. These can be anything. So Lynn asks two others in the class what they got, one said a feather and one said a key. Then she gets to one of my friends (who was one of my cards) and she says "pink dummy and engagement ring in a blue box". These presents were the same as mine. As a betting man, I would say the likeliness of that happening is one million to one.

No, more like 15 billion to one.

Thank you for correcting me.

What did the meditation show you, my son?

That I could connect to the universe through spirit.

Do you think you are special?

Yes, I do.

I don't mean that kind of special, I mean your connection to the universe.

Well when I first started yes, but as I increased my knowledge I found out that everyone has a sixth sense but it is down to free will and belief to develop it.

How did you feel after your first meditation?

I felt healed, for the first time since the age of ten sex was not important to me, it changed from sex to making love.

What have you learnt on your spiritual journey?

Not all spirits/humankind are equal.

All of you were created equal, but your development, as you call it, has been a result of free will, and you need to expand on the last answer.

From my understanding you get different levels of spirits, low and high. The low end you don't want to communicate with as they were not the best when alive so in spirit they would still be numpties.

I think you are misguided. There are no such things as low-end or high-end spirits. Every spirit is unique, and the universe or the creator (me) does not categorise them as this would be counterproductive to the end goal. What I can say is, some spirits need more healing and love than others; again it is down to free will. Some spirits want to live in despair and self-pity, fearful of the love and the light. Scared of rejection, even though the universe rejects none and loves all. Ask the question.

Why would spirits communicate through people who will only hurt and manipulate us?

You are referring to your own personal experiences. Spirits are not good or bad, they are humans in their true form. Could you ever see your life without spirits?

Not at all, I smile and laugh and feel the love of spirits. The universe blesses me on a daily basis.

How long did your healing take?

In my eyes it's an ongoing process, the healing never stops.

Now let's take the last sentence and change one word: "In my eyes, it's an ongoing process, the *enlightenment* never stops." You were never broken, as to break would mean that good and bad exist. Only two things are universe-created: light/enlightenment and love.

I read in other books, how do you love if you have never hated? How do you know you have won if you have never lost? Yin and yang.

Again, humankind has misunderstood this concept. What creator would create in their own image to punish their creations by giving them free will and then punishing them for acting on free will?

The creators only value two things: enlightenment and love. So feel free to love everything around you. No balancing act needed, none of that "don't laugh too much otherwise you will cry", "if you have pleasure you must have pain" - these are all manmade in an effort for the human mind to understand everything around it.

Chapter 4 – The True Price of Forgiveness.

I thought you said everything in the world was a god-given right? So why are we paying for it now?

Who said anything about paying? I only mentioned a price, as the price is free will. What do you think true love is?

Drinking two cans of Tennents or Strongbow (alcohol), then out with my mate on the lash in Walsall town and then enjoying a nice kebab in the evening.

This is not a joke.

One of us has to enlighten the morning, lol.

Back to the subject. I want you to explain your love story and how it developed.

What if I don’t want to?

Then my son our journey is complete, and you can burn in hell.

Was that a joke?

Does hell sound like a joke to you?

What happened to free will?

Who is lacking humour now?

Such a bad joke, bit like grandad humour. Let me get us back on track, the worst part is I have to think of how many girls I have actually loved.

Don't include the ones you "loved for one night" or the ones that you told you loved just to get them to drop their pants.

I genuinely feel outraged. I loved all of them.

Just list how old you were every time you fell in love.

18, 19, 21, 22, 24, 27, 30 and 31.

You seem to fall in love with every woman you meet.

Really? You actually want me to defend myself?

How many women have you met?

Over 1000.

How long does it normally take you to fall in "love"?

Three to ninth months.

Since feeling the love of the spirits how many of them would you say were true love?

None.

Compare universe love to the love you had.

Can I use your phrase, a billion times a billion? Lol.

Let's be realistic.

Okay, it was around ten-fold.

How did this make you feel?

I was looking forward to my physical death so I could be returned to spirit form, as the love you feel is actually out of this world and you would not compare it to anything.

And then what happened?

I started to work on myself, healing and enlightenment. Actually dealing with the aftermath of my childhood, rather than just burying it deep inside. I learnt what needed to be done.

January 19th, 2016, sitting in a guided meditation class, feeling guilty for the pain and misery I had influenced on people around me. I went to work on my badge of guilt, i.e. I used to wear this badge with pride as in my head I deserved everything that ever happened to me. Once the badge had gone the healing circle was complete and my enlightenment started.

What did your spirit guides say to you?

My true love was now coming and she would be with me in the next five minutes. Exactly five minutes after guided meditation had finished at 10.05pm, I get a text message from a girl that I had messaged twice in November, and the spirits said, "She is the one."

When did you know you were in love?

Two days later I knew I was in love. Logic could not explain how I felt.

What message did I give you at the time?

"Enjoy the journey." At the time I found that when the creator communicates with you, you do not understand it.

What was the price of love and forgiveness you paid?

A lifetime of healing, true redirection of the mind, meditating every day, unconditional faith in a greater power, or as some would call it, blind faith.

The whole terminology of blind faith is misunderstood. I don't need you to have faith in me, but have faith in yourself. Humankind rejects the thought of having faith in oneself as this means humankind is responsible for its own destiny. Humankind has always enjoyed blaming others for being too fat, too thin, marrying the wrong person, for being too poor, for being too rich.

Okay, I think I get what you are saying. We blame others for the way they make us feel.

Yes but that is misguided as well, as humankind has free will. Therefore, you are responsible for your own actions.

Okay, I accept that we are in control of our lives and what occurs in them through the power of the universe. But we all have had someone that hurt us. A broken love or a bitter love that we need healing for, or a person we have to forgive.

I will ask you again: how many women have you really loved?

One.

Has she ever hurt you? Or broken your heart?

No, but it's early days.

Do you think she will ever hurt you?

No, not at all.

Why not?

As my spirit guides have shown me a future that is amazing.

What would you do to ensure that future?

There is nothing I would not compromise to ensure this love.

Why do you feel that way?

I honestly believe that she allows me to feel heaven on earth, it is the purest form of love I have ever had. At times, it is on a par with the love of spirits/universe.

Why are you smiling, my son?

Because I look at the life I have now and it's genuinely amazing.

What is today's date?

April 3rd, 2016. Why?

So, one year and four months after you had a failed suicide attempt. Not that spirit was going to allow you to do it. You have turned your life around.

Hold up what do you mean "spirit would not allow me to do it"? I thought the creator, universe and spirit were one? And free will was the currency of choice, so if I want to kill myself I can.

The creator created the universe to help humankind evolve.

I get that part. I thought spirits did the creator's bidding to help humankind in physical form evolve?

Spirit is humankind in true form, but spirit needs a physical body to evolve spiritually.

That makes no sense at all. So spirits need a human body to evolve, I am shaking my head. One of the dumbest things you have ever said.

How do I explain this to you without ruining everything you believe?

Who cares what I believe, what are you going to say? This voice could all be in my head and I am actually crazy.

What if I said the spirit world is a bit boring and being in human form is more fun?

I would say fuck my life, as I have been looking forward to my death and now I want to live forever. You really have just pissed on my bonfire.

See, now you want to live past the age of 86 and live forever. But with no reflection or appraisal period, you would never evolve spiritually.

I feel like you prepped me up by talking about how great my life was just to kick me down, damn you, creator.

I see you still have your sense of humour, even if the people around you don't understand you.

Well I am sitting here in India and most of the people don't get me, they run around thinking they are doing god's work and it frustrates me. But I do now accept that everyone does the creator's work in different ways.

That's a whole new chapter to come. Now let's get back to the topic. The true price of forgiveness is accepting you are in control of your life. Once you

accept that, the blame shifts from other people's hands to your own hands.

So now instead of hating others you want us to hate ourselves. Well done.

Child, let me finish. Once you accept the words that you speak, they affect every aspect of your life, and I don't mean the words that you vocalise.

Even the words in your own mind play a huge part. See, the universe manifests whatever you want. If you believe love is hard work, love will be hard work. If you think you are too ugly to love, you will only attract people into your life that make you feel ugly. If you think you are unlovable you will only find people that are not worthy of your love.

Can you just give us a blueprint on how to find love?

No, and you don't find love, as you are always surrounded by true love.

Come on, stop being so cryptic.

The miracles of the universe are all around you; they radiate true love. So the price of true love and forgiveness is opening yourself to accepting true love and forgiveness. It's time to see the universe how you were meant to see it.

What if you are blind?

That's not even funny, but most of the time a blind person sees more than a person whose eyes are open all the time. Why are you frustrated?

Well, it's kind of off-topic. I read other people's work and it contradicts what I am writing and what I believe.

Most writings on behalf of the creator are written for profit. And that kind of thinking has no place in history as it was written in a way the author thought people wanted to read.

Okay, that makes me feel better.

No, you can't add your own bit about love, as it might be misunderstood, and a blueprint would contradict free will.

How about I use free will to write what I believe is the fastest way to achieve true love?

You really are stubborn?

Is that you judging me?

No, me asking a question.

Lol, so Mannu's guide to finding true love 101.
Love yourself, know your own self-worth.
Forgive yourself for the past failed loves.

Just write it.

Get an STI test to make sure it's only love you will be spreading.

That did make me laugh, son.

Who said I was joking, lol. Stop shaking your head. Okay, step three is an option. Feel the love of the spirits and universe. Aspire to only settle for the highest form of love, true love.

Only one thing I want to add, love the people you hate and want to kill.

Really? You've got to be kidding me.

Chapter 5 – The Art of Forgiveness. Thu shall love my enemy.

I shall love my neighbour.

Have you met my neighbours?

Yes, I have, and I love all my creations the same.

Even the ones that don't deserve your love?

I created humankind in my image. To not love humankind would be as painful as not loving myself. No, that picture in your head is incorrect.

Lol, the picture of the creator masturbating, making love to himself is amazing.

I have no need to have sex or to self-pleasure.

I thought you said making love was a way of heightening your emotions.

Yes, for humankind and human spirits, but creators have no need to heighten their emotions, as they are one with emotions. In this universe, we are everything but nothing at the same time.

That really does not make any sense.

Well, my son, it makes no sense as humankind's spirituality is still aspiring.

So let me get this right, as we aspire to become creators we at one point will stop having sex?

Yes, you are correct. As you will no longer need to heighten your emotions.

I am really considering regression in my spiritual path, no sex! I can't see my life without it.

But one day you will.

I feel sad.

Don't, my son, as it will be a glorious day.

I am looking forward to it (as I roll my eyes).

I saw that.

I know you did, so what is the art of forgiveness?

It is exactly what you said it is, it's an art of forgiveness. Picture some of the best art you have ever seen: how much time, practice and patience was needed?

Not really an art fan but Banksy is talented, I would imagine he has been "painting" all his life and practices a lot.

Forgiveness is the same. It takes time, practice and patience.

I understand that. I know why forgiveness is important but the whole love your enemy, love people you don't like, I think it is one step too far, this might have worked in the 70s for the hippies but in the real world it doesn't work.

But why does it not work in the "real world"?

I can't speak for all of humankind, I can only speak for my own experiences. How can I love the people that abused me? That's just tapped (stupid).

But those who hurt us the most are the ones that need the love the most.

Okay, do you mean us as creators or humans?

Humans are made in the image of creators.

Does that mean creators can be hurt?

All creators have aspired, the same as humankind will.

What do you mean aspired?

Creators at one stage of their lives were where humankind is in its spiritual journey.

So no one is born a creator?

Yes you are correct, no one is born a creator, but creators are created through the process of spiritual evolution, or as it is more commonly known, enlightenment.

So who gave birth to you? And where did you come from?

Being as honest as I can be, no creator knows where they came from or where they are going; we have but one purpose.

What is that purpose?

Enlightenment.

So how does playing "creator" bring enlightenment?

Who said it does?

So really you could be just fucking with us and when you have no more need of us, you could easily just abandon us, as this is no longer your path to enlightenment.
A father would never abandon his children.

Fuck off, happens all the time, don't you watch Jeremy Kyle/Jerry Springer?

Let me finish. A father never abandons his children. Even if he abandons them in physical form, he will always return in spirit form.

Okay sorry, I should not have told you to fuck off.

Secondly, even if the creator abandons his flock, i.e. his children, the universe is created in such a way that humankind's enlightenment would continue.

But you said that it's the creator's hand that guides humankind to becoming more enlightened.

Yes, it is, but truth be told, humankind now knows enough about itself spiritually through religion and other activities such as prayer, meditation and inner channelling that it requires no aid from the creator.

So if we require no more aid from you, what are you still doing here like a bad smell?

That made me smile. I don't smell - love has no smell or taste. I am here because I want to be here.

Are you trying to say you are here through free will?

Yes, I am here through free will.

This is just so fucking stupid. So the creator who created our universe has no idea where they came from, or where they are going?

You are misinformed on both parts. We know where we are from and where we are going.

You are fucking nuts, you just contradicted yourself!

Okay let me simplify it. As creators we know we are spirit-based energy, so yes, we know where we are from.

What?

We are from the universal energy that powers all the universes, ours included, but we don't know who created the universal energy.

Okay, that makes sense, same as humankind we know we were made from a big bang but we don't know where we are from.

You are created in the image of the creator using the universal energy.

Well, you're going to say that.

No, that's fact.

Next phase, you're boring me.

We know as creators we are heading towards further enlightenment, but we don't know what is there once we get there.

Why did you not just say that in the first place?

I did.

Okay, I'll simplify it for it for you. You know where you were born but not how you were born, you know where you are going but don't know what's at the finishing line.

As creators, the same as humankind, we were born from the universal energy, but we don't know who created the universal energy. And you are right: we know the currency of the journey and that is enlightenment, but we don't know where the finishing line is, or what is at the finishing line.

So why not stop the race?

Because the race is all we have. Without enlightenment we have nothing. What are you thinking, son?
It's a bit deep for me, it's 11.30pm and normally it's a quick wank (masturbation) and a bit of porn.

The creator shakes their head and rolls their eyes.

I smile.

I do love your sense of humour.

So is humankind running the same race?

Yes you are; you are running the race of enlightenment. Remember when I said I would give you the final piece of the jigsaw? Here it is: we are all running the race of enlightenment.

Does that mean if I'm not first I'm a loser?

No, it's a race no one can win or lose. The truth is, us creators are not even sure the race can even finish.

Fuck lol, so I might be putting in all this effort to become a better person and achieve enlightenment and it might be to no avail? I may as well become a wanker and enjoy life.

And did being a "wanker" earlier on in your life bring you happiness?

No.

So why would you go back to that place?

I don't have to try lol, it just naturally happens.

You do make me laugh. So how about you forgive and love the people that hurt you the most, as this would speed up enlightenment.

So you want me to love the guy that gave me anal as a 10-year-old because that sounds like I liked it and want it again.

As creators, we were where humankind is, at the tipping point, but we had no guidance, no creator as such to speak to. We have lived through the pains that humanity is suffering so our teachings are to reflect this.

Teachings sound like a blueprint or guidance. What happened to free will?

You will always have free will, the same as you have free will to write this, others will have free will to read this and a lot more will have free will to implement what they learn from this book. Like all the creators before me, we give the facts. How you interpret it is down to you.

Okay so once upon a time in a galaxy far away...

No, this is not a film!

Lol, okay so a long time ago you experienced how it was to be human?

Yes, I did.

Did you like it?

I would not be the creator I am today if it was not for those experiences.

But did you enjoy it?

I enjoyed the journey.

What was the journey?

The journey of enlightenment has different stages. Infant - discovering one's true self - this is the stage humankind is at.

What do you mean, true self?

Okay, I have a question for you, son. Would you say 100% of the population believes that there is more to life than physical form?

No, I would say a fair few million don't believe in a greater power.

So the first stage of enlightenment is for humankind as a collective to discover that there is more to life than its physical form. In every physical lifetime, this would allow humankind to truly ask the question, what is humankind's true self?

Okay, so what is humankind's true self?

Give it a few billion years and you will find out.

What comes after infant stage?

The creator stage.

Do we get to play god?

I would not use the words "play" or "god". You become creators.

Does that mean I can create my own species?

Yes and no. A creator through choice always creates a species through their own image. So yes, you put in the parameters, but it is the universe that does the building and maintenance. Let's say the creator is the architect. But as you know sometimes, how it looks on paper is not what turns out to be.

I can't wait to make a species out of all fit woman, Whohooooo LOL.

As creators, you do not sleep with your creations.

I know that, I just want unlimited masturbation material.

That's one thing you are not lacking in your life.

Lol, so I need to love the people I hate the most? Hmm let me try it, I love the people that abused me, I'm not going to lie I'm going to struggle because nothing positive came from my abuse.

Can you honestly say nothing at all?

Okay due to my abuse I become sexually active from a young age, I ended up having sex with people later in life I did not even want to have sex with. But you do become better the more sex you have. In hindsight, it is not really a huge benefit being good in bed.

Okay, let me break this down for you. Because of your abuse, you could not hold down a loving relationship, and a high likeness led to your divorce, which in turn led you down the spiritual path. So if I give you a choice between no spirituality but no abuse, or abuse and spirituality, which would you take?

So you're saying I have to be abused to be spiritual?

No, not at all. That's just the path you took.

Well, I would take it in my ass all day long as a 10-year-old (sounds so wrong) as long as I had spirituality.

So you could come to a conclusion that from your abuse, comes the path of spirituality.

So you could say a good thing did come from my abuse, but to love them might be a step too far.

That's because humankind has not truly grasped the concept of love.

What do you mean?

Love is all and nothing at the same time; it does not take only one form.

So what form would it take in my life, as I have forgiven but just struggle to love?

That's where, my son, the gratitude of forgiveness comes in.

Chapter 6 – The Gratitude of Forgiveness.

Let's carry on from the last chapter. Would you say you are grateful for making contact with spirit?

Yes, I am, I say thank you every day.

Do you think there is a possibility your abuse sent you towards a path of spirituality?

Yes, I accept that my childhood does and has influenced my relationships with myself and others. So yes it could have, so let's say it has.

So, my son, are you grateful for your abuse?

Fuck no, I don't care how many times you say it, whatever way you see it, it doesn't make sense. Yes, I am grateful for spirits, but I am never going to be grateful for the abuse. No way.

See how hard you find the concept of forgiveness and love towards the people that have hurt you?

I put my hands up, yes I do struggle. It goes against most people's beliefs. I get the fact that if it was not for my abuse I would not have found spirituality and we would never have this conversation, but to be grateful for the pain of my past and love them, no chance. You're really pissing me off.

Good.

Is it like you want me to abuse you?

Not at all my son, because the frustration you are feeling is what 99% of humankind right now would feel. But now you understand why it is so important to start to work on these barriers.

Why not pick an easier task?

As creators we do not choose easy or hard tasks, we choose the most rewarding task with the end goal in mind.

Okay, you need to leave this one with me as I'm not ready to thank my abusers or the cock in my ass as a 10-year-old.

Then our journey is done until you change your mind.

Where the fuck is free will in that? So basically either deal with it or fuck off. You sound like a hypocrite.

Not at all, there is more than enough content in this book to get it printed and make a difference, but now you choose how much of a difference you want to make, as this journey is your choice. Stop looking at your phone; time is not important. Either we deal with your past together, or we set a new path for humankind to follow, or we part ways.

I'm really struggling, I really am.

Your personal struggle symbolises humankind's struggles. Now you should understand how important this is to others reading this book.

Okay, let's do it. I finally accept that my child abuse had to happen for this was a manifestation of my mind, this led me to disastrous relationships as an adult which in turn lead to my divorce which led me to become spiritual.

I can't do it, I really can't do it, I'm sorry.

Son, have the strength to write the words and mean it.

I am grateful for my child abuse, as it showed me a better way to live my life.

I know that really hurt, but how do you feel?

Angry, as I feel like I have been forced.

So let's work on this tomorrow.
[The next morning]

How do you feel?

As if my heart has been emptied and a load lifted off my shoulders.

Do you still feel angry?

No I don't, I feel sad more than angry, a bit confused as well, like I am in a state of detachment from any feelings and feel like I am looking outside in, kind of empty.

Like us, humankind has spent too much energy on matters that could be resolved quickly. Hurt, pain,

anger and resentment are all emotions that work against the true emotion, love. Love is the only carrier of the universal energy.

So if you know all these other emotions are not needed why allow them in our design? Yes, I understand free will and all that but save us the heartache, will you?

Humankind was designed in the image of a creator. As creators we have experienced all these emotions, and we had no guidance, so we decided that when we excelled at becoming creators we would give guidance to our flock, so to speak.

But if you had no guidance how do you know you were supposed to become a creator? How do you know you're not working against enlightenment?

The truth is we actually don't know if it supports enlightenment or not, but as energy-based organisms we are drawn to energy. As creators, we found the universal energy grows when more love is in circulation, but negative emotions have an opposite effect.

So why not create a species that can only love?

We tried that and it had no effect at all on the universal energy. As soon as free will is removed, the universal energy stops being affected, which in turn then leaves that universe useless.

So how many universes have you discarded over the years?

We learnt from our mistakes quickly. Only a few universes were disregarded, but they continue to grow on their path of enlightenment and will become creators in their own time.

So how many of your creations, flock or whatever you want to call them have become creators?

None.

So why carry on with the process?

Hope.

I can't really argue with that.

But it's not hope as you think. Pure hope is only generated through the gratitude of love and forgiveness, which is the true foundation of enlightenment.

I am struggling with this concept, as I thought love is what made the universe go round?

Yes, but there is more than one form of love. Here we will focus on the gratitude of love and forgiveness.

Okay, you need to explain it better.

The universe works on what you think; it gives you what you think. So if you think positively it will give you positives. If you think of love it will give you love. If you think of forgiveness it will give you forgiveness.

Okay, so similar to other books I have read? They talk a lot about gratitude.

Yes and no. The core foundations focus on gratitude, which is good, but they don't focus enough on the gratitude of love and forgiveness.

Okay so explain the difference?

Having gratitude for things like money and health is noble, but humankind's focus should be solely on love and forgiveness. So the next time you feel love towards anything, let's say the love of spirit, show gratitude; love for your favourite shoes, show gratitude. Do I need to go on?

No, but what would you say is the best way to show gratitude?

By expressing love, feeling genuine love. Yes, saying thank you helps, but when you feel love towards what you are grateful for is worth a billion thank you's.

You can see where I am going with this one lol, I wake up every morning and say thank you for a great sleep, but how am I going to love my sleep? And how do I forgive my sleep lol?

Easy. Just recall a moment when your sleep was really poor. Then feel the love and gratitude for your sleep and forgive yourself when your sleep is poor. Love your health regardless of what condition it is in, as it could be worse. Love the fact you are still alive in physical form. Love your financial situation as it could be "worse". Love the

food and water you have, and if you have not eaten or had a drink for days, picture the last time you ate and drank and love that moment. Do you need me to carry on?

No, but to summarise, you seem to be going on a bit at the moment, gratitude is best expressed through love, saying thank you is the baby step and loving the good things is the advanced step?

Yes and no. Yes to saying thank you is the baby step, no to love being the advanced step. It's more the medium step, and the advanced step or stage is detachment.

Okay, what do you mean by detachment?

The best way to explain it is by using very extreme examples. So when a person becomes rich, I mean really rich, when they have more wealth than they can spend in ten lifetimes, they no longer need wealth, but due to the fact they no longer need something they will keep attracting wealth as the gratitude for money is still there but no want exists.

In the same way, a person who is overweight might not want food but they will keep attracting food.

And in the same way a happy person is so happy they don't need more happiness but will carry on attracting happiness. So what happens is the human spirit becomes detached from what it already has, but remains thankful.

So as humans what we need to do is, firstly be thankful for what we already have, secondly love what we have and then thirdly not want it? And this will make sure it remains in our lives?

Yes, you are correct. Please do use the example of a relationship?

So in a relationship you find love, you are grateful for the love but then you decide you no longer need it?

Yes, the human body and mind are made to become complacent and take everything for granted. That's why the vast amount of the population wants an easy life.

But to me, that would feel like you are taking love for granted?

Not at all. The relationships that work are the ones where you find new things to love the other person for. As you enjoy each other's company and memories made together this will give you more reasons to love each other. I'll give you an example to help you understand. When you were six and your mom brought you sweets how would you feel?

I would feel happiness and more love as I loved sweets lol.

25 years later, if your mom brought you sweets would you still feel the same kind of love and gratitude?

Yes, I would as I am a fat fucker.

No, I am being serious.

So am I, everyone loves sweets. But yes you are right I would not be in love with the sweets now as I was when I was a kid.

All loving relationships work the same; ask most couples what they love about each other now compared to 30 years back. The love evolves, as naturally the human spirit becomes complacent and takes things for granted.

Okay, question, how would you stop detachment?

You can't stop it, it's an essential mechanism in the circle of your physical form. As if you did not detach you would not want to return to the universal energy to evolve spiritually. You would want to stay and roam the earth in spirit form.

So we have a choice after our physical death?

You always have a choice; that's what I have been saying since the start of time itself!

What if I wanted to live forever in physical form, could I?

Yes, you could, but as times change and your loved ones pass away, your thinking changes and how useful you are in your own mind actually changes. As your self-worth changes so does your life span.

That's actually really sad.

But it's an essential part of the evolution of humankind.

So if the reflection period is important, why not reduce our lifespan to 25 years and condense what we learn?

Because that would affect free will, and in some lifetimes you actually learn nothing new but just enjoy the journey.

How come sometimes it feels like we are living through the same lifetime over and over again?

Déjà vu is feeling what you felt in another lifetime, but no lifetime is the same, as every reflection period/appraisal pushes you towards more enlightenment.

So if I suddenly decided to become a murderer and kill hundreds of people how would that push me to enlightenment?

How do you know you have never murdered anyone?

I hope not.

Just because it goes against what you believe now does not mean in past lifetimes you have never behaved in certain ways, as social norms have changed over hundreds of years.

I don't understand.

Okay, 5,000 years ago it was quite "normal" for a 10-year-old to get married.

So are you trying to say 5,000 years ago I used to be a paedo?

No, son, because 5,000 years ago that behaviour was "the norm".

So, 5,000 years ago everyone was a paedo?

Do you actually think in 15,636 lifetimes you have never been a murderer, paedo, rapist, or involved in mass genocide? And do you think you have never been raped, murdered, mutilated, hanged, shot or stabbed? Think you have never been a son, daughter, father, mother, uncle, aunt? Do you think you have never been famous, rich, poor, fat or hungry?

Okay stop, I get it, we have lived out every possibility.

No, as if you had lived out every possibility there would be no need to come back to human form.

Fair point, so how many possibilities exist?

A billion times a billion times a billion.

Wow that's a lot of lifetimes to get through.

Yes, it is my son. So may I ask you a question?

Nope, but you're going to ask it anyway.

Why did you stop writing this book for the last three months?

Self-doubt, pain, and all the things I have tried to run from for the past 30 years. Well, you could say all the things I am trying to run from now.

But your struggles are the same as most other humans. You really do underestimate how many millions of people will relate to your book. It is time to change the world and the universe at the same time. Ask the question.

What's the difference between soul and spirit?

The soul is earthbound and does not leave the body; it's the vessel for the journey of the spirit.

So why do we need both?

Imagine going on a picnic with ice-cream on a hot summer's day. Without the cooler box, the ice-cream would melt. Now picture that the soul is like the cooler box and it's essential for the spirit to travel in.

So the soul is more of a storage component?

Not a storage component. More like the CPU of a computer. Without the soul, the human body would not work.

Would the human body work without the spirit?

Yes, it would.

Are there human beings alive that have no spirits?

Yes, there are.

What is their function? To make up the numbers?

No. The spirit can choose when to leave the body.

Can the spirit leave the body before death?

Yes, it can.

What happens when it does?

It has happened, many times before, and it will carry on happening.

Can you give examples, please?

Let's say the body and brain enter a vegetative state, i.e. a coma, and there is no chance of recovery. The spirit may choose to move on as the soul will carry on fighting to survive, and with modern medicine that is now possible.

So are you saying if your loved ones are in a vegetative state we should let them die?

Not at all. As we have seen throughout history, miracles have occurred where vegetative-state individuals have made a full recovery.

So are you saying it's a choice?

See a lot of writers are mistaken. They take the spirit and soul as one thing. The soul is a box in which the spirit can fit. No, it's not your brain.

What organ would you say it is?

The soul would be best described as your heart, and as you know, if your heart stops working you can get a transplant.

So if the spirit is in the soul and soul is the heart, if you moved the heart would the soul move with it?

No, I said the spirit can fit in the soul, but I did not say it remains there at all times.

So what would you describe your spirit as?

Your feelings. How you feel is your spirit. And no, this is not the end of the book, just the end of the chapter. Our work is not done yet and never will be done. Have a nice day, son.

Chapter 7 – The Pain of Forgiveness.

Firstly, let me tell you how proud we are of you. I know sometimes you don't get the praise you want, and even when you do, you don't acknowledge it. We are taking note of all your hard work and it's helping the universal energy move in the right direction. But it is time to step it up. What is today's date?

16th August 2016.

How many weeks has the first part of your book been out? Stop checking the calendar, it's been six weeks.

Yeah you're right.

Of course we are right. Six weeks, and how many people have read your book?

A few thousand.

What more do you want?

I want to change the world.

Not your burden to bear.

So you want me to be happy with helping a few thousand?

Son, you should be grateful for changing one person's life. You're on a crusade to change the world: why?

I feel like I have found a rewarding path where I can help people change for the better. So yeah, I want to help the world.

Okay, not to piss on your bonfire, so to speak, but firstly you're not Jesus, or any of the other messengers I have sent. Secondly, even they never put so much pressure on themselves. They decided to help one person at a time and they were happy with every person they helped.

So you're making me write a book, which from the feedback is actually really good, but you don't want me to get it out there? Did you bump your head whilst I was gone?

No. I want you to be happy with the here and now and stop putting so much pressure on yourself. What if I was to say your book would make a bigger difference once you're gone?

Give me a gun and I'm coming now my lord lol.

No one wants to read a book about an atheist who met a greater power and then killed himself. And what is with the title? It sounds like a sloppy love story, "The purity of love".

Author note - that was the original name for the first six chapters.

Well where were you when I needed a name?

If you had listened, your book would have never been called The purity of love.

Ffs now you tell me lol, going to be hard work to change it now.

Don't worry, by the end I'll give you a deserving name, something that will reflect the book. On a side note the sub-title is worse than the title. "When an atheist meets his maker"?

What's wrong with that?

Firstly, there is no such thing as an atheist; everyone at some point in their life believes in a greater power. Secondly, I am the creator - technically your mom and dad made you.

Okay how about I change both parts? Happy now?

Son, free will tells me to tell you to do what you want, but if you want to change the world, change the title.

Okay point made. So you start off with how proud you are and then give me a verbal beating like no other.

That was no beating, but we are proud of the man you are becoming, and that lovely woman you're going to call Mrs Mannu. We really like her.

You keep saying we? You found a Mrs Creator whilst I was gone?

No but your book sent shock waves across more than one universe, so it got other creators interested in the outcome.

Fuck me, so my book sent shock waves across universes and you're crying about the title?

Not crying, giving hindsight.

Okay I promise to change the title, happy now?

I am always happy, son. You are really becoming a man that every parent can be proud of.

Yeah sticky subject.

We know. That's why we are going to write this chapter, The pain of forgiveness, and no son, that is not the new title of your book.

But I actually like that name, it sounds cool.

No.

Okay, should I start, or you?

Fire away.

So I can honestly say I am no longer a wanker, I am actually a nice person, trying to make the world a better place, but just feels the nicer I am the quicker I get dragged to the gutter.

Do you have any specific moments in your mind?

So me and my mom have a proper explosive relationship, youngest child, proper mommy issues as my ex-wife would say lol. Don't get me wrong, lovely woman, unconditional love but somehow we end up pissing each other off, and since I've become a nicer person I refuse to be pulled into the drama, but somehow I manage to get myself dragged in with both feet. And then we ignore each other for a few days which actually upsets me and makes me cry, to top it off my grandad, her dad, comes to me in spirit form to confirm she is being stubborn etc. Tells me I should just let it go, in the end I just end up crying like a little bitch.

You are no longer a little bitch, so you are safe, but in all of this what confuses you?

How is it I do so much good, but still end up hurting? I mean when I was a bad person I kind of deserved it, so I kind of accepted the pain as karma, but now I'm golden balls and I still get hurt. How does that work?

You were never bad in my eyes, son; the guilt you carry you no longer need to carry. Did you know a lot of humans have "mommy issues", so to speak?

Ermmm, because they still got the umbilical cord connected and don't know how to be independent men?

No, not at all, mommy issues are not gender specific. The connection a mother has with her child during pregnancy is misunderstood.

Well you better explain it, as you did say that one of humankind's flaws is the child is born at conception and not at birth.

Yes you are correct. Do you know why a lot of humankind has mommy issues?

Well if I did, I would be able to resolve mine, so no I don't know.

The reason is, most of your fears as a human are the same as your mom's.

Most of your core beliefs are the same as your mom's.

So the reason why a lot of humankind doesn't have a healthy relationship with their moms is due to the fact they are so alike.

I disagree, I'm nice she is not, so how the fuck are we the same?

Does someone have mommy issues?

Well according to you, if you don't have mommy issues you're not normal.

So mommy issues and anger?

Not at all, so to solve my mommy issues all I have to do is change? Bam done.

It's never that simple, my son.

Why not?

Because years of negative energy and negative thoughts are going to take more than a split second to resolve.

Can I be brutally honest?

Yes you can son.

This chapter seems a bit of an anti-climax compared to the others.

Well the other chapters were more emotionally damaging to you, as these issues were on the surface and they were easier to identify. The issues in this chapter are under the surface and harder to identify.

So get on with it, what are my issues under the surface?

Learn to walk before you can run. We first have to learn, understand and forgive our mothers for the beliefs and sometimes the pains they gave us.

So how do we do that?

We regress to when you were conceived.

You sick fucker, I don't want to regress to when my parents were having sex.

How about when your dad's sperm was chasing your mom's egg?

How about one week after that?

Okay let's go with it. So we will regress to that moment using meditation.

Hold up, most of the readers will not know how to do this.

That's true, but after reading this they will find someone that can help.

Okay my suggestion, make sure it's someone that has qualified to do regression.

I agree, someone not skilled in guided meditation might do more damage than good.

So whilst I am in the womb what do you want me to do?

You my son are going back to the womb to find out what your mom was feeling whilst pregnant, and what she ended up passing to you as emotions and feelings.

After an hour.

So what did you feel?

In the womb I felt fear, loss, guilt and a sense of not being good enough.

Now can you reflect on those emotions and say in your childhood and adulthood you have never felt these?

I think a lot of humankind would feel those feelings.

But let us talk about how those feeling affected you.

From the outside you could say they never actually affected me.

It's okay to think that on the surface, but a lot of your deep-rooted feelings are based on the time in the womb.

I actually can't be fucked right now.

Okay I'll ask you: what are you frustrated with right now?

I feel like my life is static. Feels like there is no movement the way I want it to be. Feels like I am writing for the sake of writing.

You keep spending time and energy on stuff that actually does not matter, but due to free will we don't interfere.

I get that, but it feels like I have so much more to offer and now I am kind of hitting my ceiling.

I am glad you brought that up. Let's go back to how you felt in the womb. You felt a combination of fear, loss, guilt and not being good enough. So how do you feel now?

Okay my fear, the next chapters are not going to be as good as the first six chapters.

But no matter what you write, this is not for you to judge, as you are a mere vessel. This book will make a difference long after you have left this life and this physical form.

But there is so much expectation now.

Who cares about the expectations? Ask yourself, is it expectations or the fear of not being good enough?

A mixture of both, with a hint of guilt.

Don't you think it's time you forgive yourself for all the people you hurt?

I am trying to, but I feel like my ego is holding onto my old me as it's scared of change.

It's not your ego that is holding on, it is your sub-conscious, as holding on to the guilt makes you feel as if you're not good enough. That's where your feelings come from.

Okay, let's focus on each one and you tell me what comes to mind. Let's focus on loss.

I am scared of losing myself, sometimes I feel like I am regressing on my spiritual path. I feel like I am going backwards.

The saying "you have to go backwards to go forwards" is misunderstood. It does not refer to this life, it refers to regression. Having a glimpse of the past helps you move forward. As you look into the past you see life keeps repeating itself. Different times, different places but still the same outcome.

So then in this lifetime you realise it actually does not matter; that way you take away the stress and focus on the inner core. The inner core only cares

about one thing, which is love. So does it actually matter?

Let's talk about this year's targets you had.

Which ones?

The financial ones.

Okay so January 2016 my clean break order comes through and my aim was to buy my own house. We are now in September.

Okay, where are you at now? You're at the point of getting your third property. How do you feel?

Well soon as I got the one, the goal changed to 10 and I would be more content with 10.

What was your target in your love life?

I wanted to meet the person who I would spend the rest of my life with.

We brought into your life not just your soulmate but your spirit mate, and then what did you do? ***(Read the next chapter to see the difference between soulmate and spirit mate.)***

I wanted to get married asap.

So the goal posts moved again? And what about your enlightenment?

I wanted to be able to channel and give readings.

Can you now do that?

Yes I can.

Once you were at that level what did you want next?

I wanted to be able to feel spirit, see spirit and communicate through their physical form rather than telepathically and feelings, which in turn would allow me to make a difference to millions.

So the three key factors humankind judges itself by. Love, finance and enlightenment. Your targets changed every time you achieved them?

Yes they did.

So the new goals you set yourself, what are you going to do once you meet those targets?

Most likely move them again. But everyone does that, it's called goal setting and motivation. I want direction and the feeling of achievement.

Once you do regression, you will understand that you have done this nearly every lifetime. Then you have a eureka moment and realise why you constantly set goals and targets.

All of humankind sets goals, achieves them and then sets even bigger goals. Then the circle comes back around to a moment when the goals are so big that they can't achieve them and then they feel like shit.

So you're trying to say we should not set goals?

Do you know why humankind sets goals?

To progress in life, to achieve, to develop and to become more.

In whose eyes are they becoming more?

Yours, ours, maybe everyone's?

Okay. I actually don't care, as I am not judgemental, but I gave free will for humankind to do what it wants. So how do you become more in your own eyes?

Once we achieve our goals we become more than what we were before we achieved them.

No. As your goals change so does your mindset. As you have a new goal to aim at, so you start working towards it.

The "everyone" part I'm not even going to answer as it's stupid, since no one actually cares if you hit your target.

I disagree, our loved ones, friends and family want us to hit our goals.

Okay, why do your loved ones want you to hit your goals?

Because they understand how important they are?

No, they want you to hit your goals because they think it will make you happy. They actually don't care about your goals, they care about your feelings as they love you.

I am sure me becoming rich would be a goal my loved ones would love, especially if I share the money.

You are right, but then it stops being just your goal, it becomes a collective one.

I don't understand.

Okay, a husband and wife share everything, and husband has a goal of making ten million pounds. Suddenly it's the wife's goal as well as she knows she will get half of it. Second example: you want to run a marathon, your wife does not care about you running the marathon but supports you as she knows it will make you feel happy.

Okay so I understand that, don't set goals as they are the bringer of evil and destroy humankind's hopes and dreams?

Don't make me start on the evilness. Here is the moment that every reader will understand. You set goals not for the happiness you get when you achieve them, but to feel like you are not good enough while you're trying to achieve them.

Fuck me that's actually true.

Now you understand why it is important to go back to the womb in regression and work out

subconsciously what was passed on. Here is the worrying fact: 99% of people set goals.

Give me two minutes.

Lol, you do make me laugh. Tell the readers what you just did?

I just deleted every goal on my phone. I am now ready to be goal free, and yes there goes the mood board lol.

How about we change the mood board to not what you want, but what you already have, and instead of wanting more you just say thank you for what you have every time you see it.

So you want me to stick photos of where I am now? A bit vain?

How about sticking a photo of you, your family, your loved ones, your bank balance, where you live, the car you drive? That way you can just say thank you every time you see it.

Thank you for the guidance.

You still misunderstand the purpose of this book. Yes, it's your guidance, but more importantly it's humankind's guidance.

So now after the meditation I understand the subconscious and how it made me feel, it made me feel as I was not good enough.

So what have you decided?

I am never going to make goals and targets, as they make me feel as if I am not good enough.

Okay, what's the next feeling you want to address? Take your pick: guilt, fear or loss?

Let's go with loss.

So your mom is in a generation in which a lot of children died young. After losing two children and having two miscarriages your mom became scared of losing you.

So how does that manifest in my life?

You are constantly fearful of losing your way. After years of being on a destructive path you now feel you are on the "right" path but are constantly fearful that you will regress or become that "bad person" again. A bit like an alcoholic who thinks they will start drinking again.

So how do I stop it?

Easy. Stop worrying that you think either path is right or wrong and start living in the now. Enjoy today and stop worrying about tomorrow. Stop putting so much pressure on yourself.

That's easier said than done. A lot of humankind has the belief of guilt.

But why do you feel guilt? Because you fucked around with girls and hurt them? Sorry for being the bearer of bad news. You were not all that, as

they have now all moved on. The only person that has not is you, and that's because you feel guilt.

Hmmmm.

"Hmm" does not make the guilt go away; it's time to forgive yourself. You have paid the price for your so-called sin many times over; now reap the reward of your labour.

What does that even mean?

Think about everything you have dreamt about, and more is on the other side of the door: the door of self-forgiveness. Is it time to walk through?

You are right, it is time to stop punishing myself, and I have paid my debt.

The sad thing is there was no debt to pay in the first place. Okay, let's focus on fear.

What are you scared of?

My own shadow.

Lol, if you were scared of your own shadow, you would not have been such a cunt.

Ermmm I shall not judge?

That's not a judgement, just the truth. So it's okay for you to make a joke but when I do you get your knickers in a twist?

My jokes are funny, yours was just mean.

Well I think it was funny. You just don't have a sense of humour.

Okay, I'll go buy one, hahhaha, better?

No, you are boring me now. At this moment right now what do you feel?

Rejection.

So, would you say your fear is of rejection?

I have a huge fear of rejection, thinking about it, I don't even know why, it's a bit scary.

The worst part is, rejection is what motivates you.

I don't understand that statement.

Look back at everything you think you have achieved and it will link back to your fear of rejection.

Why did you learn to cycle?

Because I wanted to get away from my family and cycle really quickly away from them and run away.

Stop being a drama queen.

Okay I wanted to learn to cycle as I did not want my dad to love me less because my older two brothers could cycle.

So would you say fear of rejection from your father was a strong reason to learn how to cycle?

Yes it was.

Okay let's move on. Passing your GCSEs and A-levels.

Rejection from my mother.

Putting weight on.

Rejection from my wife-to-be.

Okay, side note, we actually really like this one.

Thought you don't judge?

We are not judging. Sometimes things just don't work. Humankind has always tried to fix everything; just accept somethings don't work.

Okay, so how do I stop the fear of rejection?

It's simple: what are you being rejected by and for what?

I actually don't know, my mind is blank.

So let's work out when was the last time you were rejected and for what.

I actually don't know.

That's how simple it is.

Okay I'm really confused.

As soon as you accept no one can reject you and there is nothing to reject, it all goes away.

So all I have to do is accept there is nothing to reject? That seems too easy and simple.

Okay let's try again: in the last four weeks have you felt rejection?

No I have not, all I have felt is love.

That's the only thing you should feel. Now, to explain the difference between soulmate and spirit mate.

Chapter 8 – Soulmate

How come it feels like that last chapter finished prematurely?

It kind of did. See, my son, we are going to come back to it later on.

When?

A bit impatient this morning, are we?

Don't know, kind of feel frustrated but not in a sexual way.

Lol, you never feel frustrated sexually, I wonder why you never feel sexually frustrated?

Eyes back on the prize, I shall not judge?

Do you remember what you used to say at university?

I used to say a lot.

Okay, I will remind you: "There are two types of wankers in the world: the ones that admit it and the ones that don't."

Yes I thought it was funny until I met a wanker who would not admit it, he then got all weird on me, like I had put a finger in his ass whilst he slept.

The word you're looking for is, he became uptight.

Or he behaved like I had finger-fucked him whilst he slept and secretly he liked it.

Lol, lets stick with your definition.

So why did you bring the whole wanker subject up?

Firstly to lighten the mood after the last chapter (mommy issues) and secondly it's significant in reference to the difference between spirit and soulmate.

Okay I am lost, what's wanking got to do with spirit mate and soulmate?

Not the wanking part, the part where some admit it and do it and some don't admit it and deny it.

What's to admit? Or not to admit? I really do have a confused look on my face.

You get different levels of love, the highest being true love. This is made over millions of years and focuses on the spirit level. This is what all entities aspire to have. Lower down you get soulmate love. You look so confused.

Because if it does not make sense to me then the readers are fucked.

Let me simplify it for you. Spirit love is what you have when you meet your perfect partner. As soon as you meet this person you know this person is the one.

I thought you had multiple "the ones" or is that just me who falls in an out of love lol.

You have multiple spirit partners but over time it becomes one spirit partner.

The start of the sentence sounded like a script from a porno film, multiple spirit partners lol.

Just for ten minutes can you get your head out of the gutter.

Okay done lol.

You don't have multiple spirit partners at the same time, but as you take time learning to bond "over time", you will choose one.

So after you have chosen "the one" then what?

Then you come to the playground which you call earth. You come to earth to feel pain, love and all the feelings a physical existence can give.

So we come to earth to have sex?

Not just sex, but to be able to touch, to feel and to feel alive.

So in spirit form we can't do that?

In spirit form all you can do is communicate.

No sex in spirit form?

No.

Please my lord I don't want to die or get old lol.

Stop being a child.

But it's true, the more you tell me the more I don't want to die.

I'm just going to ignore you. But you can keep writing if you want.

Like I have a choice.

So the spirit mate is the one; the soulmate is a lower level of love. As we discussed before, the soul is the animal instinct in humans. It gives desires such as reproduction, to feel love, to eat etc.

If the soul is the bringer of evil, why do we even need it?

The soul is essential for life to continue on earth, as without the soul, sex would not be enjoyable and half the "mistakes" in the world would have not been born, and over time humankind's physical form would have become extinct.

But what about the issue of overcrowding? Lack of resources etc. to maintain life on this world?

The earth can sustain ten-fold more than what it already holds.

80 billion?

Nope, more like 100 billion. The population is closer to ten billion than the eight billion you think it is.

So where are the two billion hiding?

This is where, my son, your thinking is limited. Eight billion physical bodies and two billion spirits.

Two billion dead people, that's a lot of fucking ghosts lol. Why don't they just move on?

Resentment, guilt, judgement and many more reasons. The biggest issue is lack of forgiveness of themselves and loved ones. In regard to how much life earth can sustain, once humankind is on the verge of destruction it will look towards the stars for answers. That will help humankind come out of the infant stage.

Will humankind find aliens?

What would be better than aliens?

Finding god?

God is not to be found, but discovered in one's self. Back on topic, humankind will find civilisation on Mars, but it will not be aliens, it will be humans.

This therefore will indicate humankind lived on Mars till its destruction and then moved to earth. But on Mars there was no infrastructure for humankind to travel. The questions it will raise will be very challenging. But they are the right

questions for humankind to progress to the next stage of enlightenment.

Well that will be a long time after I'm dead, so can we get back on track? I understand the difference between soulmate and spirit mate but don't understand the correlation with my wanker joke.

When you meet your spirit mate you just know. But when you meet your soulmate it takes time to come to the conclusion of love, and the brain comes to that conclusion. Let's use your ex-wife as an example. At the time you were looking for someone that was good looking, Indian, academically intelligent and would get on with your family.

Yeah you're right.

So when you met your soulmate, were you in love straight away or did it take months?

It took a few months. So is my spirit mate the one I fall in love with at first sight?

No, that's called lust. Let's use your present partner as an example. Did you love her without meeting her?

Yes I did, but in the real world that is stalker-ish and god damn weird lol. If a mate come to me and said that, I would slap him and tell him to go watch catfish.

Did you love your partner/wife-to-be, sounds a bit better, before you met her?

Yes I did.

Did it matter what she looked like?

Well if she was not her and was a man called Steve, I might have struggled.

The only reason you would have struggled was because of the lies and being let down by someone you love.

We're just going around in circles.

Did you like your wife-to-be before you started to love her?

No, I actually did not know her when I started loving her.

That is the difference right there. You love your spirit mate without knowing why you love them, as you don't even know them. But with your soulmate, you have hundreds of reasons why you love them.

That's actually quite deep for a Friday morning.

Do you know why a race of males and females was created?

So we can have sex?

No. The male and female are needed to create energy. In the same way as with electricity, male and female current is needed.

Okay, but what is the end goal of love?

To become one. The true purpose of enlightenment is to become a creator.

You said that already.

Do you remember asking if there was a Mrs Creator?

Yes I do and you said, “No, but I don’t lack companionship.” But how is that relevant?

So a creator is born when a male and female spirit become one. That is the highest level of enlightenment we know.

Does that mean you are asexual?

No. Nothing in the human dictionary or thinking can label me apart from the word “creator”.

So over time me and my spirit mate will become one?

Yes, but don’t worry, you’ve still got a few billion years to get there.

Well that makes me feel better, the more spiritual I get the less sex I will have.

Trust me on one thing, true enlightenment will make the emotion of sex feel like sorrow.

That doesn’t make sense, talk straight English.

I'll dumb it down for you. True enlightenment is like driving a Ferrari whilst sex is like driving a Ford. And no, it does not depend on what Ford it is!! Just take that as it is.

Lol, okay so what is better? soulmate or spirit mate?

Both are as important as each other.

But you still have not explained the correlation with my wanker joke.

You're not going to let it rest, are you?

No I'm not because it feels like you are side-stepping my question.

That's because I am, as it will infringe on free will, and no you can't just make it up as you see fit.

Well what other options are you leaving me with?

In reference to two types of wankers, the ones that admit it and the others those that don't, soulmates are the same: the ones that admit it's not true love and the ones that don't.

Hmm damn, a lot of people aren't going to like that.

Yep a lot of people are going to have a long deep look at their own lives.

Are you trying to get me killed?

No not at all.

I can see a crazed husband whose wife left him after reading this book coming to kill me.

Trust me when I say, 86 is when you will leave your physical life. You have too much work to do.

I can feel the pain of the readers as they read that out and realise they are missing out on their spirit mate.

The truth is, most will think, after reading this, that they are with their spirit mate and their exes were their soulmates. So if anything you just gave them a false sense of security. So, well done for that.

Was that a dig lol?

No, not at all. What would this book achieve if 90% of the world found out they love their soulmate and gave up on their spirit mate?

Most would feel like shit?

Yes and this book is not to make people feel shit, but to help them forgive themselves and others around them.

So how would they forgive themselves in this situation?

Out of 100% reading this book, 80% will ignore this part as they believe they are in love with their spirit mate and they will get confirmation they made the "right choice", or they are single and

realise that past relationships did not work as they were with their soulmates and not spirit mates. So 80% of readers will be happy with this.

Now let's work on the 20%. 10% will think they are with their soulmate and have made the wrong choice, but they don't have to be so tough on themselves.

Why not?

As 80% of the readers love their soulmate, what harm really comes from it? None, as they will just come back again and have the opportunity to love again.

So 80% of our love lives we will love the wrong person?

No not the wrong person. Your love will simply not reach the levels it could.

So we covered 90% of the readers, what about the other 10%?

The 10% are the ones that think they have lost their spirit mate to death, life or other people.

So basically where they don't feel the same way or have died?

Well for that 10%, as you have mentioned, we have good news. Your spirit mate never leaves you once they meet you. Even in their physical death they never leave your side.

That doesn't help a grieving wife who lost her husband does it? Even if they come back in spirit form?

Humankind is so blind. You often hear news of how one partner dies and then suddenly the surviving partner dies as well within a short period of time.

Yes we do, kind of sad but good at the same time.

Your physical life on earth is linked to your spirit mate. When one physically dies so does the other.

Woohoooo, I'm so going to get killed, I can see my death by a disgruntled widow, saying how dare you tell me my dead husband was not the one.

A widow holding onto her dead husband is not forgiving oneself to encourage moving on with life?

True.

So let's say even if the last statement was false and spirit mates are not linked, would you not want your loved ones to move on?

Of course I would.

So let me state it again. To all the widows out there, to all the woman and men who think they have lost their spirit mate. Keep loving, as the best is still yet to come. Time to forgive yourself and move on.

Feels like a closing chapter statement.

Yes, it is.

Chapter 9- The roles our parents play

Okay, you may not be able to relate to this chapter, but it essential for children who have been abandoned by their parents to understand the reasons why their parents did what they did.

But why would they need to understand? Are you going to justify shitty parents?

No, I'm not here to justify but to enable understanding, so healing and forgiveness can take place.

From the outset I can tell you that a lot of readers are not going to be ready to let go of poor parents. I have heard so many stories of children losing their parents to alcohol abuse, drug abuse, parents not ready for the responsibilities and even losing their parents to new partners. Just sometimes feel there are so many unwanted children.

But it's not just dads these children have been let down by; they have let themselves down as well.

So you're trying to say these children deserved shitty parents?

No, not at all, but they have allowed the past to control their future. All the issues they have had because of "poor parents" have resulted in resentment. A bit like your child abuse, which resulted in you holding on to your guilt. These children have limited their own lives.

Can't use poor parenting and child abuse in the same context. Two different things.

Why not? Because you think your child abuse is more important than someone having "poor parents"? There is no such thing as a poor parent. That's why I am using speech marks, as to call any parent "poor" is to judge. But let's just go with the comparison.

Okay, I do think my child abuse might have been a bit more traumatic than having an alcoholic father or druggy mom. I think they just need to get over themselves.

Everybody's pain is different. It's unique to each person. How individuals deal with it is a choice, but we are not here to judge.

Okay, but it's so frustrating. Truth is, I don't even see my child abuse as anything big any more. I see other people get wound up about it, I just think they should let it go.

You, my son, need to understand that everyone is at different stages in their own spiritual path.

Will humankind ever get there?

Yes they will, give or take a few billion years. Ask the question.

Is there other life in the universe?

Yes, there is.

How come we have not met them yet? I'm looking forward to finally meeting E.T.

Because nothing will be gained by humankind seeing a flying saucer and little green men. It's much easier for aliens to be born into human bodies through their spirit and integrate with humans to make a difference.

How many aliens are there on earth?

One in every million humans is an "alien". They chose to take physical form on earth to encourage enlightenment.

Do these people know they are aliens?

They work it out as they get older; they feel as though they don't understand human nature and they feel they don't fit in.

Were Jesus, Mohamad and other messengers of the creator aliens?

Yes, they were. They had their own enlightenment to enrich, which was to help another species evolve on its spiritual path.

Were they successful?

Depends on what you call a success?

Stop side-stepping the question, did they achieve what they wanted?

No, but in reflection every "action" helps humankind towards its long-term goal of enlightenment.

You do know this is going to sound way too out there?

Okay, think of your lifetime so far. There is always one person that sticks out in your mind as one in a million, and something about them makes them stick out. No, I don't mean in a sexual way either.

Lol.

Personality, charisma, love, something will make you take notice and then remember them years on.

Okay I agree with that, but to say they are aliens will scare a lot of people.

The term "alien" is misunderstood. The word should mean any life force that has lived on multiple planets. Different planets are at different stages of enlightenment, so life forces/spirits will go where they choose to and believe they will have the most rewarding experience.

I feel a little better, but still a lot to take in.

Let me re-state what I said: when I say "aliens" I don't mean little green men.

Okay, I get it. But how did we go from shitty parents to little green men?

Because it all relates.

How?

Different planets have different levels of enlightenment, so some of the species that are now in human form have come from less spiritually developed planets - you would say they have taken a step up. So, like anything new it's going to take them time to adjust.

So let me get this right, you're saying shitty parents are shit because they are aliens?

No. In the terms you're using, they are "shitty parents" because they don't have the experience older, more enlightened spirits would have.

Still feels like you are defending shit parents and drug abuse and alcohol abuse etc. Just feels like bullshit, so you're trying to say it's okay for young inexperienced spirits to be arseholes?

Substance abuse is no excuse and a lack of experience is not an excuse either. But let me simplify it. A lot of this is to do with the immaturity of the spirit.

Is that a judgement?

No not at all, just a statement of fact that the more experience a spirit gets, the less it becomes reliant on external love and focuses more on internal love. Okay, let's tackle them one at a time, otherwise we will carry on in circles. Let's start with fathers who abandon their children.

Owwwww a sticky topic, I likey.

Once the baby is born the mother starts to give more love to the child than her partner/husband/father of the child. The father, due to lack of love, will start looking elsewhere to find it.

I have seen partners that have cheated whilst their partners were pregnant.

The above still applies, but the process has speeded up. The husband/boyfriend stops feeling the love from his wife/girlfriend. As she starts giving the unborn baby more love, he feels neglected.

So if the female gave more attention to their partner it would be okay?

No, not at all, as that would result in the wife/partner etc. mothering both child and partner.

Is it so bad if she mothers both?

Not good or bad, but she should not need to. The main issue is humankind has still not grasped the true meaning of love. Love is not taken or given. But it is from within. You can't control how much love you get but can control how much love you give. This would be so much easier if you just wrote it down instead of typing it.

On a timescale, get going. Have football. Come on.

Most of humankind reacts due to the lack of love in their lives. The issue is not the love they get; it's the love they give out. But as they are empty on the inside, they don't have a lot to give out.

So you're trying to defend men that leave their kids?

To defend would be a judgement of right and wrong. But I'm explaining what you asked.

That does not help the healing process for lots of people out there.

The book is not about healing; it's all about forgiveness.

But don't they kind of lead to the same thing?

No, they don't, as forgiveness is the key to life.

I thought love was?

Have you ever seen a person love freely who carries guilt? Resentfulness? Or a person who is full of hatred?

I can't talk for humankind, only personal experiences.

You have to forgive your way to a better life, my son.

Is that the title?

No its not.

So let me get this right, without forgiveness we can't as humans have a complete life?

Do you understand the power of forgiveness?

Yes, it means you feel better once you forgive people or events for all the pain and misery they put you through, and yes I know you forgive not for their sake but for your own sake. But can I be honest, sometimes I just don't want to. Fuck them, let them burn.

The worst part is that even after all my teachings of the past humankind still struggles terribly with forgiveness.

Okay, let me stop you there. I have two takes on this. Sometimes we do not want to be the better person, why should we when it's the other person's fault? Then when you do forgive these people they shit on you multiple times. You forgive them and they do the same thing again, so what's the point?

Son, do you not understand how important forgiveness is? It is the foundation to all enlightenment. No enlightenment can take place whilst one suffers from guilt.

How does lack of forgiveness result in guilt?

The deep-rooted truth is that humankind has evolved enough to understand that they should forgive. The problem arises when humankind fails to forgive and they feel guilty for not being "the

better person". This is the early stages of resentment.

I don't understand, how is this the early stages of resentment?

Deep inside you have this competition in which you have to be better than yourself and others around you. This results in you wanting to be the better person, and one method of being the "better person" is by forgiving people who don't deserve it.

I get that but where does the resentment come from?

Okay, let's simplify it; shall I draw you a chart?

Well Kindle doesn't support charts.

Okay, so you feel pain, and the person who hurts you gives you two options: to forgive them or not to forgive them.

That's not a flow chart.

I'm just going to ignore that. So you decide not to forgive them, and after the initial pain you feel angry and resentful. That's how resentment is built up.

What happens if you forgive them straight away?

Do you actually think humankind is enlightened enough to forgive straight away?

Well I think I am, nothing actually gets to me, well most things don't.

Okay let me stop you there. We are talking about forgiveness, not tolerance. Okay do you remember the last argument with your mom?

I have so many lol?

Okay, the one two weeks back, when she stopped talking to you for four days.

Well, I did nothing wrong, so I had nothing to beg forgiveness for.

Okay, but when you were not in "the wrong" how did you feel that your mom never spoke to you?

It really pissed me off.

So now you understand the difference between having a high tolerance and forgiving someone.

So I have to forgive when I am pissed off with someone or some circumstance, but having a high tolerance is when things don't affect me?

Yes. Having a high tolerance does make your life easier, but does not make you immune from resentment.

Okay I get it.

So when your mother had "wronged you", how did you feel?

I was pissed off with her, slightly angry as I knew I did fuck all wrong.

So after being angry and then resentful, what did you do?

I did not really feel resentful, more pissed off.

Okay. Describe how you felt after the initial argument?

Pissed off, told you that five times, can't you hear me today?

Are you having a thick moment? I'm trying to dumb it down for you.

Stop being a twat.

Well my son, stop lying then.

Okay, after being pissed off I was resentful. Happy?

Why were you resentful?

In my head all I thought was, if I had a relationship with my mother like my older brothers have, she would not react that way.

So you're resentful of the relationship your brothers have with your mother?

I don't think resentful is the right word to use, as that would be borderline jealousy.

But son, can you honestly say that sometimes you're not jealous of the relationship your siblings have with your mom?

Honestly not jealous, not resentful, just want to be treated equally.

So how does your mom not treat you equally?

Well like I said, if she treated us all the same, then we would not have a problem. I can assure you she treats us siblings all different.

But what do you expect?

For her to treat us all equally.

But why should she?

Okay two reasons, one, it's the mother's job, second, it's the right fucking thing to do. How hard can it be to treat all your children the same? Does not require rocket science.

You are "right", it does not require rocket science, but I'll ask you a question: do you treat your parents the same?

In what way?

Are you really trying to side-step the question?

Yes I am. Lol.

Really, son?

Okay, I love my dad more than my mom, happy?

This makes no difference to me. Why do you love your dad more than your mom? Both are biologically your parents, so you should treat them the same.

Okay, can you stop with the bullshit and get to your point?

No point, just a question: why do you love your dad more?

I got lots of reasons why I love him more; want me to list them all?

No, there is no need. So all the girls you have dated and slept with, why is it you never treated them all the same?

As some of them never deserved the whole of me, some of them were hoe bags, some just wanted dick. So how would I treat them all the same?

So two key relationships in your life and you don't treat those people the same?

No I don't.

Do you treat your friends the same?

No I have my favourites.

The truth is, sometimes you do more for your friends than your own mother.

The sad truth is you're right.

Let me stop you there. No sad truth, just truth. To be sad would indicate right or wrong.

What's the point you're trying to get to?

Humankind expects to be treated "fairly" without practising what they preach.

Okay I accept that, but what's that got to do with shitty parents leaving their children etc.?

It has everything to do with "shitty parents". In your eyes they are "shitty" because they never behaved the way you expected them to. But the truth is they behaved how they wanted to, in the same way as most choose to treat people differently.

So praise the fucking lord, let's forgive shitty parents as they were exercising their free will.

Being a bit dramatic, are you?

It has been a tough week, you just made me realise I am a shit son.

A lot of readers are going to struggle to forgive "shitty" parents, but holding onto the past is a one-way ticket to an unhappy life.

Yeah I get that, but the truth is a lot are not ready to let go. I can feel the pain of the readers.

Son, is it the pain of the readers or your own pain?

Think it might be a bit of both, but my pain has nothing to do with this chapter.

Is that you making a judgement on yourself?

Not at all.

So how do you feel, and why has it been such a tough week?

Two weeks back I got attacked on a football pitch.

And?

Defended myself. But felt guilty for the pain I inflected on the other guy. It would have been easier to let him punch me and feel the physical pain compared to the pain of the guilt.

So, son, let's re-word that last paragraph. I felt guilt for the pain I am going to inflict on my unborn/child. It would be easier for them to never know me than let them know how much of a "shit parent" I am. How do you feel now son? Still think your life does not relate to this book?

I feel like crying and just hugging all the parents that let their children go.

The biggest reason why parents abandon their children is they think the children will be better without them in their lives, because their own value is so low in their own eyes. So even though this chapter was written for children that have been abandoned, it's time for the parents of these

children to forgive themselves. So far this book has focused only on the "victims", not enough on the parents, rapists, paedophiles, murderers and "bad people" etc.

This will be a tough subject to cover, as most of the world would want to see these people burn.

The worst part is, son, one chapter would not be enough to cover it.

So at least I know what one of the chapters is going to be about.

Not yet, son. We have not covered this topic in enough depth. Ask the questions and I'll answer them.

I am struggling, as we have covered alcoholic, druggy parents. We have also covered why moms and dads would abandon their children. The main focus has actually been why parents have to forgive themselves and children need to forgive their parents. Anything you want to add?

Yes, my son. Even in your darkest moments you find strength. You think that you're leaning on us for support - how misguided you are.

Why am I "wrong"?

We look at you and others like you and are so proud of the direction that humankind is heading. You don't value yourself as highly as you should. You spend most of your life helping others find

their own true worth but then neglect your own self-worth.

Thank you, but how does this help the readers forgive?

The readers see your value and they understand that if such an inspirational young man can have self-doubt so can they.

Chapter 10- Knowing your own value

What is today's date?

You're the Almighty lol, you tell me.

I know the date; I created time itself. But the readers don't.

What difference does it make what the date is?

Why are you getting so defensive?

Because I know what's coming!

You mean, what you think is coming? The creator does not have any desire to criticise you. So I repeat, what is today's date?

23rd November 2016.

When are you looking to release this book?

Ideally January 25th 2017, with a pre-release of two weeks, so it needs to be all done by the 10th January.

How many days does that leave you?

61 days.

Do you think you will get it done?

I think I will, but don't know about the quality of the content. Writing shit is quite easy.

Why do you think the last two chapters will be bullshit?

Who said I am only talking about the last two?

You do make me laugh. Behind all this bravado lays the truth.

What's the truth?

You are scared, my son.

Scared is an understatement. More like petrified.

But why?

Fear of being killed, ridiculed, where do I start?

Firstly, no one is going to kill you for writing a book, humankind is no longer at that level of enlightenment.

Okay, so I don't get killed, but I get ridiculed for being a weirdo who got abused and now talks to dead people. That's even worse!

Yes son, you will get ridiculed, but that's only because they misunderstand you, and are not at the spiritual enlightenment level needed to understand. This book is not about the here and now, but for the masses of the future.

That's okay for you to say. But as a human I kind of want to see the world change.

Do you actually think after your death you will be going back to human form any time soon?

I don't know, sometimes I feel like I am done and everything weighs me down.

The struggles you're going through I have seen before. Many, many times.

And that's going to make me feel better?

No, not at the moment, but this will: the bible was first written in 15,000 BC. The teachings still live on now and will carry on living on. The original message has changed over the generations, and will carry on evolving as humankind does.

Okay. Let me stop you there, what is the message?

Are you asking for yourself, or are you asking on behalf of the readers?

Both?

If, at this point, you and your readers have not grasped the teachings in this book, then you are not ready for the enlightenment.

Stop being grumpy and just state them before I make them up.

Forgiveness, self-worth, love and enlightenment.

The forgiveness, love and enlightenment I was expecting, but self-worth? And before you try and be funny, I know the title of the chapter, knowing your own value.

Self-worth is as important as the others. I will demonstrate. I will use you as a live example. What is the title of this book?

Ermmmm, Purity of Love (old title).

No, son, what is the title we gave you a few days back?

Power of Forgiveness.

No, what is the title?

Makes me sound crazy.

Why?

I don't want to be seen as a high and mighty type. I have seen it so many times, just because they pray or believe in god they think they are better than you and talk down to you.

I'll ask you again, what is the title of the book?

The Forgiveness Bible.

Now what is the issue you have with that title?

Actually makes me sound like a whack-job.

Is that before or after you confirm to the world that you speak to spirits?

To be fair to you, when you say it like that I am surprised I have any friends or family left. Never mind a loving wife.

She is not your wife yet.

I know that, but she will be.

How do you know that?

Because spirits and my intuition tell me.

Let's focus on the intuition part, as intuition is humankind's basic connection with the divine. Before you become spiritual and could connect with a greater power, how many times did you get a "gut" feeling that something was wrong?

All the time, I mean after all the stupid things I did, I never actually got hurt. Even before connecting with spirit I believe I was looked after by a greater power.

Do you believe in god?

I believe in a greater power, but religion lets humankind down, so I don't believe in god.

Why does religion let you down?

As you said, it has evolved but I don't think it has done enough. When you look at the world around us and how much wealth, power and influence religion has, I don't think they hold themselves as accountable as they should.

What would you want them to do?

I am sure they have enough wealth and power to reduce poverty, hunger and conflict. But they seem to spend more time preaching to deaf ears or enlightening themselves through meditation and praying.

What are your priorities in life?

After connecting with a greater power, I would say my priority is to enhance my own spiritual journey.

What else would you like to do?

Help others find the path that I am on.

So technically you are doing the same? preaching to deaf ears and solely focusing on your own enlightenment through meditation.

You're actually right. Fuck I have become what I have feared the most, my mom.

You do make me laugh, my son. Your mom is actually lovely, but you do not see her value. The sad thing is you will never see her value until after her death. But that's a chapter in itself.

Get back to topic please?

The problem you have, and most of humankind has, is that you think your way is the only "right way".

And before you say it, I do understand, son, and I have seen you become more respectful of other people's religions and beliefs. But do you think you have done enough?

Yes and no. From where I was, yes, but for where I want to be, no. A lot of deep-rooted hatred towards established religion. But looking at it now, I do the same, so I have no leg to stand on.

You do know that every messenger of the creator has been ridiculed one time or another in their life?

Okay, there is a difference between being ridiculed and humiliated.

Every messenger of the creator gets ridiculed, but the truth is every human gets ridiculed. That's how humanity handles its lack of self-worth.

So you're trying to say humans ridicule one another because they do not know their own self-worth?

Have you ever heard the phrase, "What you see in others is what others see in you?"

Yes I have, basically when someone pisses you off, you look to see why they have pissed you off and that's what you need to work on yourself.

Okay, you misunderstand the quote. If you only have negative thoughts about someone, that is all they will see in you, as pushing out negativity will return to you 10-fold. So let's use your example of religion. You make a judgement on certain

individuals within a religion that you think are trying to get one over on you or you think they think they are better than you just because they are "closer to their god".

I can't be the only person that has met a smug priest etc. I have seen it in multiple religions, the teachers of the religion are so smug because they think they are better than you.

But son 99.9% of humankind think they are better than their fellow human beings. It's like they are in competition with each other.

Do you blame us? From a young age we are told to better ourselves and are constantly being compared to others, making us want to be better. But it gets even worse, the sad fact is when we are not competing with others we are competing with ourselves.

It's not just humankind that has done this. Other species have been through the same stage.

So what is the solution to the problem?

Enlightenment is the key, but humankind is a few million years away from getting to that point.

Too vague, need to be more to the point.

Okay, most of humankind compares one another, but have you ever asked the question why?

It's in our nature?

No, it's not in your nature to compare, or to try and be better than your fellow man.

Okay, so what is it?

Jealousy.

I don't compete with the next-door neighbour's kid because I'm jealous, I can assure you of that.

Your thinking is too narrow. Let me explain: how many times have you watched someone on TV and said, "Look how good he or she is at football, but I bet I am better than them at colouring." And before you say it, football and colouring are just examples.

Okay, I am guilty as charged, I see footballers on TV and do think "Wow how good are they," then I think, "Why am I not that good?" And then something inside me will tell me I am better than them at xyz.

Do you know why you have those thoughts?

Because I like making myself feel better in imaginary situations and to stop making myself feel like a loser.

Okay, but why do you feel like that?

Because criticising myself sometimes brings pain to the surface.

Let me break it down. Who told you that you were not as good as xyz at football?

No one really has ever told me that, but don't get me wrong, I just get the feeling I'm shit at football lol.

So all this time you have compared yourself to footballers on TV and criticised yourself?

Yes I have, but let's be honest I can't be the only one that thinks I am shit, otherwise I would be playing at a top level.

How is anyone going to have belief in you, if you don't have belief in yourself?

I do have belief in myself, especially with things I know I am good at.

But son, the only person putting a judgement on whether you are good or bad at something is you.

Let me give you several examples. A kid at football rejected at a football tryout, an individual at a beauty pageant rejected by judges, anyone that has sat an exam or did coursework etc, and never got the grade they wanted. At some point or another everyone is made to feel as though they are not good enough.

I'll answer every single example for you. A kid being rejected by scouts at a football tryout is a judgement by the scout. How many times has humankind seen these rejected players go on to make it professional?

A person's rejection at a beauty pageant is a judgement by the judge - how ironic does that

sound? But beauty is different to every individual, as humankind is discovering.

Anyone who has sat an exam or done course work etc, and never got the grade they wanted. To understand this, you have to answer one important question: who sets what grades get what? A person who never sat the exam or did the coursework in your circumstances. So how can they judge, since everyone is unique?

I am struggling with this topic, just seems a bit bullshit.

Firstly, you don't have writer's block, as to have writers block would indicate that this is your creation and your teachings, which would be incorrect. You are just the messenger/vessel.

Secondly, why does this topic seem bullshit? Because you can't relate to it?

Most of humankind has read so many books about self-worth, and how we should look in the mirror and love what looks back etc. But deep down it changes fuck all.

So why don't we help the readers with this issue?

How the fuck am I going to help the reader if I can't break out of the cycle myself?

Okay, when was the last time you compared yourself to others? It's okay, son, just say it as it is.

I feel like a dick for saying it as in hindsight it actually does not matter.

It might not matter now, but did it matter at the time?

Yes it did, it made me feel so small.

But why do it? Let's start from the beginning.

So my partner/wife-to-be is a professional. So in her job she meets wealthy, famous and rich people, everything I am not. So as she is what 99% of humankind would call beautiful she gets chatted up/hit on a lot. I can handle that, but then one guy became a bit stalker-ish, offering to take her on holiday, buy her nice things, everything I wish I could do for her. At that point I actually considered if this person could give her a better life/future than I could, as if we are being honest her future with me might not be plain sailing. Yes, financially I am okay, but this guy could take her on holiday every week for the next 100 years and still have plenty of money left over.

Sometimes we really do feel like giving humankind a slap and telling them to wake up. Do you really think your partner is with you because she wants a holiday every week? You actually think that guy is the first or last guy that has offered her "the world"?

I know I have a lot to offer, but you asked when the last time I compared myself to another person was. Even though he is richer than me I have more to offer in a loving relationship.

Okay, sorry to be the bearer of bad news, but you can't actually offer more or less than the other person.

What are you on about?

Every person is unique. What you offer is what only you can offer. No one else can offer that.

I get the whole yes everyone is special and unique, but the fact is, he can offer her a better financial lifestyle than me, I can give her love care and affection.

You are mistaken. What you need to understand is that what you have to offer is not measured in one metric.

Again with the "everyone is unique" bullshit, we get it, everyone is different.

No, my son, humankind has not grasped how unique each person is. As creators we get frustrated with humankind when it uses phrases like "I understand what you are going through".

Getting a bit random today are you not?

Not at all. The phrase "I know what you are going through" is so misused. No one can understand what you are going through as every person is unique.

Okay, let's talk about divorcees and when people use that phrase.

So every person's experience is unique to them. No one situation can be the same. Let's apply science to this: do you remember what they taught you at high school when you were doing experiments?

Yes don't mix red and black together or it would go bang.

No, not that.

Ermm, don't do drugs?

You do have a sense of humour, but your jokes are closer to dad jokes than you realise.

Lol, yes I do remember, for the experiment to be valid you could only have one variable.

So how can any situation be identical? As the person involved in the situation is unique.

Yeah I agree with that to a certain extent, but you can relate to other people's pain and feelings.

But you use the phrase "relate" - how far can you really stretch that word? Okay, the guy you met three days back, the guy that got divorced in 2013, would you say he is over it?

No, not at all, you could feel and see his pain in his eyes.

What was your initial reaction?

I wanted to hug him and tell him it's okay but I was scared just in case he got freaked out or liked my hugs too much lol.

Stop lying.

Lol, I actually thought what a pussy, it's been three years get over it already.

And what else?

That he should stop being a little bitch and acting like he's the only one in the world that has been divorced. Loads of people go through it. I have been through it.

That's where you are mistaken. No one has gone through divorce the way he has. As everybody on this world has been a million years in the making, from their first life to this life, from their upbringing to the people they interact with, it all changes them as individuals and that is the beauty of humankind: everyone is unique.

Okay so no one understands what he's going through as his divorce is unique to him. So what now? Every reader is going to feel sorry for themselves? Awwwww poor me, I got divorced, no one understands me as I am unique.

Why are you frustrated with people who feel sorry for themselves?

I don't know, but I think it's because sometimes I have moments of weakness and I feel sorry for myself.

When was the last time you felt sorry for yourself?

A few days ago my gas boiler broke. The insurance would not cover it, so I knew I would have to spend money that I did not have, and that's when I thought ffs why always me.

Okay, explain to the readers where you are at financially?

I know where this is going, I know I'm not even in that bad a place.

No, son, please explain it so the readers can see humankind's problems in the fullest.

Okay, I am tight for money as I have just bought two houses.

How much did the two houses cost you?

£40,000.

So in the last three months you have spent £40,000 and you felt sorry for yourself over a £150.00 boiler repair bill?

Okay I get it, I overreacted, cried like a little bitch and need to man up and stop being so judgmental on others! I get your fucking point!

There actually is no point. Does the last paragraph not sum up how you feel about your own self-worth? Deep down you want to fight the good fight

and be a better person but external circumstances seem to drag you down?

I do want to be a better person and I don't want to judge others, at the same time I don't want to be ungrateful, but during tough times I do remember things I don't have.

So let's focus on each one of those sentences. I want to be a better person; this is very simple, just stop judging yourself.

Easier said than done.

Son, as soon as you stop judging yourself all the negative feelings that go hand in hand will stop.

How would you suggest I stop judging myself?

Easy. Every time you think negative thoughts about yourself, just write them down, think them aloud or just say what you're good at. And before you say it, everyone is good at least one thing.

Can you tell me what I am good at?

I don't do ego enlargement. But what would be the point of me telling you what you're good at?

Make me feel better?

But son, it's not what others think you're good at, as that's them making a judgement. It's about you and what you think you're good at.

So personally I think I'm good at helping people, through my interaction I believe I help people see their real value, which most of the time is higher than what they think.

Now that you have written that, how do you feel?

No different.

So let's write what you're not so good at?

There are so many things I could list, where do I even start. Scared of being a bad husband, a bad father (don't even have kids yet), I could be a better son, brother, uncle.

Stop, just stop. So let's work this out by applying a little logic. What you're good at was one sentence and what you're bad at is a whole book by itself?

Would you say writing and saying what you're good at worked?

Don't think so, but I have read that in so many books, I thought it would work.

So let's simplify it. Don't have "good" or "bad" thoughts about what you can do.

That's just fucking stupid, look at me, I can't do anything right but woohooo I can't do anything wrong either.

Son, why is it stupid? Because you don't understand it?

I understand it, but sounds like bullshit.

Are you where you want to be in life?

No.

So do you accept that all you have done has not worked in your eyes?

Okay, I accept that not everything I have done has worked, otherwise I would be where I want to be in life.

So how about trying it my way, son?

I'll try it, but what if it doesn't work anyway?

Okay, in the words you would use, "Stop being a little bitch" and just do it.

Lol. Okay I'll stop thinking about what I am good and bad at, happy?

You actually think it's going to be that easy? You're going to have to learn thousands of years of living, but once you achieve it, it's a truly enlightened place to be. Do you understand what you will achieve once you do it?

A place of true enlightenment? Lol.

No, my son, a place of no judgement.

I am actually excited to make that journey, Really intrigued to see if it would work.

It will work, as it's worked for millions of species before humankind. And as creators we had to do this ourselves to become enlightened. Do you want me to answer the remaining statements/questions that you listed earlier?

No, but you're going to anyway.

"I don't want to judge others". This will stop as soon as you break the habit of judging yourself.

"I don't want to be ungrateful". This in itself is a judgement.

"I don't want to focus or think about the things I don't have in my life". This needs a slightly different approach as you need to differentiate between what you want and need. Is there anything you need that you don't have?

Nope, I actually have everything I need.

So the lists of wants are what?

Judgements on my own life, things I think I need to make my life better.

How do you feel right now?

A bit confused, a bit emotionless, I feel like I just found out Santa is not real lol.

Yes, you are right, son. But fact is fact, even though every individual is unique, which is something to embrace. Their own value is actually nothing in human form.

So do we have value in spirit form?

Humankind is not ready to understand the answer to that question.

Why not?

Because if humankind was at the level of enlightenment it needed to understand the answer it would never need to ask the question.

So recap the chapter. Humankind has no value?

Yes you are correct.

Humankind has no self-worth?

Yes you are correct.

Humankind is worth nothing?

Yes you are correct.

But is that not a judgement in itself?

No, son, I merely speak facts. What has humankind actually contributed to the galaxy or universe?

The only currency you value is love.

Yes you are right.

I think overall humankind has given a lot of love.

It has, but it still has so much more to give.

Give us a break?

I am speaking only of fact. Humankind has not covered the cost of creating its universe and itself. As you would say, it's in a deficit.

How long till we overcome the deficit?

A few billion years.

So why carry on? Why not just finish us? And let us die?

Okay, firstly you never die, you just evolve. Secondly, I can't just let a species die as the universe is self-sustaining.

So really this chapter is all about how humankind is worthless and insignificant?

Not at all, this chapter is all about knowing your self-worth.

Well you just told me my self-worth is nothing.

Yes I did, but did you understand it?

Yeah, I am worthless.

No, son, there is a difference between your self-worth being nothing and being worthless.

How?

Once you grasp how not to judge or be judged, you realise everything around you no longer matters. The pressure to be more than what you are stops. You learn to be happy with what you have. After all that you actually work out that you are worthless, as the contribution you make in one lifetime is so small compared to the bigger picture.

So, why are you making me write this book if the contribution it is going to make is so small?

Because a 10,000-billion-mile journey can only happen if you make one step in the right direction.

Okay, I can't argue with that.

Here is the scary statistic. It's not in every life you step in the right direction. In most you don't step at all.

So what's the point of coming back to earth in human form?

Sometimes it's just to enjoy the journey. And before you ask, no you can't step backwards, but you can step sideways. Even with sideways steps you are still learning. You seem very frustrated.

I had hopes of this book changing the world.

My son it will change the world. Okay let's say all eight billion people on earth read this book - how many would you think have the capacity to

understand it and use the principles within this book?

20%?

Okay let's go with that figure, 1.6 billion. Out of those, how many are you hoping will step in the right direction?

All of them?

Okay, you are hopeful. Just be happy if you help yourself and one more step in the right direction.

So what's the point in writing this book?

Simple. This book was all about helping you step in the right direction.

Chapter 11- No Name

Question, why is there no chapter name?

Because humankind has no word for what will be discussed in this chapter.

Why do I have a feeling I'm not going to like this chapter?

As your intuition knows, this chapter is all about helping the true victims of paedophilia, murder, rape, theft and anything else humankind thinks is "bad".

I am actually scared to ask - who is the true victim?

The true victims are the perpetrators of the "bad" acts.

Lol, I am actually speechless.

Why, son?

As you actually think the true victims are the murderers, paedos and rapists out there.

Yes they are, and the list is not only limited to those who break the law, but includes others as well.

Like who?

The person who feels guilty for having an affair, the person who feels guilty for the domestic

violence, the person who feels guilty for not helping others.

So any one that feels guilty?

Yes and no. As a large portion of humankind feels guilt for committing acts that they think are "bad".
No as some of the people who commit "bad" acts don't feel any guilt at the time of committing them but do feel the guilt later on.

Are you on about how people should repent?

No, not at all. Why do you think humankind has to repent?

To help it overcome the sins we have done.

The whole philosophy behind repenting is misunderstood.

In what way? I thought it was straightforward. Humans do "evil/bad", feel guilty/bad for their actions, then cry like little bitches for being "bad" and then beg you for forgiveness. Lol see, straightforward. That's how you repent.

Let's break down what you think repenting is. Firstly, there is no such thing as bad or evil actions. Secondly, there is nothing to feel guilty about as there is no right or wrong. Thirdly, I have no desire for humankind to beg me for forgiveness.

So all this time I have been doing it wrong. Fuck me.

No, my son, humankind thinks repenting is the key to happiness.

I don't think repenting is.

Do you speak for the whole of humankind?

Of course I don't, were you dropped as a child or something?

No, I was not dropped as a child, but I'm sure you were.

I see you are back to your normal judgemental self.

Not at all, just frustrated with you.

Why?

Because you have all this knowledge inside you, but fear stops you from truly expressing yourself.

I am scared, but what's that got to do with repenting and happiness?

Okay let's focus on repenting. Humankind "sins" in its own eyes, feels guilty for the sin and then asks forgiveness from a greater power.

I already know that part, why are you repeating yourself?

Because humankind loses focus on what actually needs to happen.

You are actually a cock, you really are talking in riddles and shit. Get to the point.

Okay repenting should not involve forgiving the sin. Repenting should be acknowledging no sin/evil etc, took place. Once that occurs, what does humankind have to repent for?

I can hear all the paedophiles cheering at that one.

You take too much of this book personally.

How the fuck else am I going to take it? Yes I have forgiven my past pains etc., but to feel sorry for a paedo, murder, rapist because they are the "true victims" here. Bollocks.

Why are you so angry?

Fuck you.

Anger is not the-

Just fuck off.

Do you still think you no longer need healing?

Where the fuck are you going with this? And no, my healing is not complete, even after writing about forgiveness for the past 12 months I still have a deep pain in regards to my past.

What part of your past hurts the most?

Honestly I can handle the part of being fucked as a kid. That part, I held no power over. But I still feel guilt for the way I treated numerous women in my life.

What comes to the surface?

I hear all these horror stories of people treating their ex-partners with such low value, as the saying is "like shit off the bottom of your shoe". And I then think about everything my partner went through and it makes me angry that somebody would treat such a nice person like that.

Then the guilt kicks in and I think, fuck that's how I treated my ex-wife, I am one of those people.

Son, you never treated your ex-wife the same. A lot of the guilt you are feeling is due to exchanges between you and your ex-wife during your divorce. When humankind is hurting, they say a lot to hurt one another. This is due to lack of love and the fear of losing love.

But that still does not help with the guilt.

What do you feel guilty about?

I think I could have conducted myself better in regards to the divorce.

Okay, how many years did you give you ex-wife in total?

Eight years.

Were you a "good" husband/partner?

Yes I was, but I feel I could have been better.

Yes, but the flip side is you could have been "worse".

Yes you are right.

Financially, who was left in a better position?

She was.

To what amount?

£100,000.

So all in all, you gave your ex-partner £100,000 and eight years of your life. What else could you of gave her?

A more dignified break up/divorce.

And how would you have done that?

Been nicer, more gentle, and taken a bit more time.

Son, nothing would have made it better or worse. It happened, now is the time to get over it.

Thank you.

What are you saying thank you for?

For healing me, I realise that I actually have nothing to feel guilty for.

Can I reflect on this chapter so far?

Hmmmm, go for it, like you would listen if I said no lol.

So your biggest problem in your life was feeling guilty as you thought you had "wronged" your ex-wife.

Yes it was.

To the outside world/readers your abuse would have been a bigger problem.

Well it used to be, until I learnt to forgive.

But if you had truly learnt how to forgive, why did you feel guilt for the way you dealt with your divorce?

Because it's sometimes easier to forgive others than it is to forgive yourself.

Okay, let's use your life's example. We will start from the present and work backwards.

Go for it.

You feel guilt for your interactions with your ex-wife?

Yes

Do you think she feels guilt?

I'm not even sure, don't understand how that is even relevant.

Son, it is.

I think she would, as I would say we both played a part in the divorce and the interactions.

Would you say you played a part in your child abuse?

Well my abuser was not fucking thin air was he?

(Shakes head in disbelief), you know exactly what I meant.

Lol, I do think I played a part in my abuse and how I deserved it, that all stopped, soon as I learnt to forgive and let go.

So right now do you think you played a part?

No I did not.

Do you think you manifested your child abuse?

As a child I don't think I had enough drama going on to manifest it.

I can assure you, your child abuse was not manifested by you. Humankind still has not grasped the true understanding of "victim" but hopefully these examples will help.

Do you think your ex-wife has forgiven you?

I hope so, so she can move on with her life.

Okay, let's go with it. She has forgiven you and moved on with her life, but you, my son, still hold onto guilt because you think you did "wrong".

Well, I feel better and I am slowly letting go.

So after three years you are a distant memory for your ex-wife - she actually feels sorry for you - but yet you still beat yourself up over guilt.

But I no longer feel guilt, thanks to you.

So who do you think was the true victim of your divorce?

Without sounding like a drama queen, I was.

But if you were the true victim, what was your ex-wife? And no, she was not a little bitch.

I would say she was kinda the victim too.

Yes she was son, you were both victims. She was the victim until she forgave you, and you were the true victim until you forgave yourself.

Okay I'm going to sound thick, but what is the difference? You need to spell it out.

In each act of "bad", "evil" etc. there are normally always two victims: the victim and the true victim. So in your divorce you were both victims, but over time you emerged as the true victim, as it took you longer and more willpower to forgive and move on.

Sounds all a bit convenient that the true victim is the one that has the lasting pain?

No, my son, not lasting pain but the one that takes the longest to forgive, as no healing can truly occur until one forgives.

So basically the true victim is the person that takes the longest to forgive?

Yes they are, and trust me when I tell you that forgiving yourself to rid yourself of guilt is much harder than forgiving someone who has hurt you.

How is it?

Simple. To forgive the people who hurt you is self-preservation, and can be seen as being selfish in humankind's eyes, as humankind is at the level of enlightenment at which it understands it must forgive others to gain control of its own life.

I agree with that and we did touch on it earlier in the book.

Also, humankind understands it can't control other people, so a person's behaviour is their choice, which enables humankind to forgive others.

But how does this relate to redemption?

Easy. True redemption can only occur once one forgives themselves for the "evil" they have done.

But that's nothing new, do evil, cry about it and then ask god/creator for forgiveness.

Okay I'll repeat myself. True redemption is when you forgive yourself. No need to ask me for forgiveness, as in my eyes my children can do no wrong. Buts it's for my children to forgive themselves. That's the true path of happiness and redemption.

Never really thought of it like that, always begged you for forgiveness.

Do you know why humankind looks to the stars for forgiveness?

Boredom lol.

No son, humankind finds it easier to put their suffering, pain etc. into someone else's hands rather than take responsibility.

To be honest, I have done that myself, instead of tackling the issues I have asked you for forgiveness.

But son, I have nothing to forgive.

Okay, what about the people that don't feel guilt, how would this affect them?

Humankind still looks at life as this life only -they are "born" and they "die". What do you think actually happens once you die?

You go party in heaven?

Okay, do you recall when I said the spirit world is a bit boring?

Yeah.

Well, once you die you spend most of the time reflecting on the life you had and deciding on what life you want next.

Okay, that it?

Yes that's it, but reflecting on the life you had might take several thousand human years. Also, as you stated, some humans don't feel "guilt", but every human will feel guilt one time or another in life.

The afterlife is no different as "death" does not give you answers but raises more questions.

Hold on, I was wanting to die so I could work out the meaning of life, and now you're telling me death will bring more questions.

Yes it will, as in death, time is static, which gives you time to reflect on your life.

So, son, are you ready to complete the healing and forgiveness circle in your life?

Yes I am.

Who was the true victim in your divorce?

I was, I now realise I no longer need to hold onto the guilt.

Now for the other guilt.

I don't have any other guilt.

I know you don't, but you continue to add to someone else's guilt.

How?

Who was the true victim in your child abuse?

The child that was forced to suck cock.

I really do feel your pain, my son.

How can you feel my pain? Thought all us humans were unique and no one can feel the way you do.

You are right, but I am not just any one, am I?

Okay you feel my pain, whippi fucking whooo.

Until I brought it up, when was the last time you thought about it?

Once a month.

How often do you think your abuser thinks about it?

Every fucking night as he pulls his dick to the thought of fucking me lol.

Behind the humour lays what?

A shit load of pain.

Just write it, my son.

Okay, I don't want to play the victim card. I'll be perfectly honest, my life is actually fantastic.

I know it is my son, but imagine how much better it would be once you complete this healing circle.

Really, I think my life is really good right now. I have a saying, you know your life is great when the biggest drama in your life is FIFA Wednesdays. (On Wednesdays me and a few friends get together to play computer games.)

I agree your life is good, and I am glad you see its value. But is anything lacking?

I lack real meaning in my life and direction, I feel a bit lost.

Okay, what do you think you can't do?

Write what you want me to write.

And what is that?

Fuck you, I am not that stupid, okay I am but not this time lol.

Stop hiding behind humour.

I don't want to write it, the true victim of my abuse was my abuser.

How do you feel, and why was it so tough?

Because I feel like I am lying. I feel like I am lying, I feel like that sentence is a load of bullshit.

Okay, let's go with it, it's "bullshit". How do you feel?

Angry and pissed off, why would the creator/god take the side of a fucking paedo over his loving child?

As the creator I never take sides; you are all my children.

Children being the pun here lol.

Okay, son, again stop hiding behind humour.

What else do you want me to do? Cry? I did that for over 20 years, why are you hell bent on bringing it back up?

Does your struggle not reflect humankind's struggle?

Okay it does, so the true victim was my abuser. Now what?

How do you feel?

Slightly lighter, less burdened but still confused as how do I know I'm not the true victim here? Not like I stay in contact with my abuser.

Trust me son when I say, not a day goes by when your abuser does not feel some form of guilt and reflects on it.

Can I ask you a question?

Yes.

How did I manifest my abuse? What kind of drama did I have going through my head to manifest abuse as an 8-year-old?

See, my son, you are now enlightened enough to understand that your abuse was not your manifestation but the manifestation of the abuser.

But being abused affected my free will?

Yes, it did. Humankind has a habit of affecting one another's free will.

I feel really frustrated, like you have not really answered any of my questions.

That's because you have not asked any questions. I'll ask you a question, my son: if you had a choice between being the abuser or victim what would you choose?

Victim all day long.

So who are the true victims here?

The ones that commit these hideous acts.

I still think you need a bit of work on this. What would you rather be, the murderer or victim?

Victim.

Rapist or victim?

Victim. I get it, they are the true victims here as they have to deal with the nasty shit they have done, but I still feel empty, like something is missing from the jigsaw.

What do you think is missing, my son?

I actually don't know, just feels like I am empty.

Can you share with the readers what conclusion you just came to?

I was never the victim, the true victim was the abuser as I would never want to be that person, as I would struggle to live with myself.

So, my son, who needs more love and guidance? The paedophile or the abused?

My personal judgement is the paedophile.

Let's take the word "judgement" out. The ones who need the most love and guidance in the world are the paedophiles, rapists, murderers who day in day out torture themselves for actions they have taken.

So what do you want to call today, hug a paedo day?

Stop hiding behind humour.

Come on, that was a little funny.

No, son. It's time for humankind to become the species that we hoped it would become: it's so close.

I thought you said we were a few billion years away?

You are, but with every step we get closer to the truth.

What is the truth?

That this life, the last life and the next only have as much meaning as you let them.

I get that.

Son, do you actually "get it?"

Yes, I do, let's live the life we want.

You are mistaken my son. You already live the life you want; you just choose not to accept it.

The truth is, I don't know what life I want.

That's because you just hit the next stage of enlightenment.

What's the stage? Being confused? Lol.

No.

The art of detachment?

No.

Come on give me a break. What's the stage of enlightenment I just hit?

What's the point of me just telling you? The journey itself is the reward.

I think I know what it is.

Enlighten me son, pun intended.

Whohoooo now you want to become a comedian.

Never too late, it's only taken me a few billion years.

Lol, is the next stage of enlightenment, not to desire the life you want as you already have the life you need?

Yes and no.

What do you mean, "yes and no"?

Yes, you are close, no, you are far.

What the fuck? What does that even mean?

What it means to you is significant only to you. Everyone is unique. Now go and enjoy the life you have, not the one you want.

Chapter 12 – Where to start?

Interesting title my son - so what's the date and where are you now?

13th of April 2018. I feel like I am where I was three years back.

Why do you feel like that?

What's really changed? Still doing what I was doing then, fucking around.

Let's start from the beginning: what has changed?

Well the happy ever after was not so happy ever after.

I'll ask you again: what has changed from the last chapter to this chapter?

Do you even have to ask? You already know!

It's not about what I know, it's about what you know and where you are at.

So the love of my life moves in, and I'm done within one day.

Explain "I'm done".

After one day of living together I knew she was not the one for me.

And how did this transpire?

In a meditation I could see the pain I would go through and the slow break-up.

So what did you decide to do?

I decided, "Why wait six months to suffer? I may as well cut my arm off now."

Would you say it was a brave thing to do?

Wtf are you on about “brave thing to do”? That doesn’t even make sense. How is it brave to make someone you care for be upset and see them cry?

How difficult was it to break up with her?

Truth be told, harder than my divorce.

Why was it harder?

Because there is me on this spiritual path, supposed to be the person that helps others get to a “higher level”, and I can’t even get my own shit together.

What was the hardest part?

Looking like a complete twat, writing a book about love, how purely I love, and after one day breaking up with the girl that inspired the book.

You do make me laugh, son.

I am fucking glad you find it funny.

This book was never finished. This book is about your journey and how it will inspire millions.

Right now, I want to be the better person and say this is what I want, to help millions to a better life, but truth be told no matter how much I lie to myself right now, all I want is pure and true love.

But son, you already have that.

Yeah yeah, we are surrounded by love, heard it all already.

So, son, I'll ask you again: where are you now?

Everywhere and nowhere.

Stop trying to be a smartass.

I feel like I am where I was three years back.

Why do you feel like that?

Because after the break-up, I went wild again, but this time it was worse.

Why was it worse?

Because my manifestation was to a whole new level. I don't even know what's the point of adding to this book. Maybe the illusion of the happy ever after is better than what's to come.

Still don't think what you are doing is brave?

Stop talking in fucking riddles. Spit it out, will you.

Son, if you want, why don't you stop writing? You do have free will.

Fuck you, you know why I can't.

Because your ego and arrogance will not let you.

What fucking ego and arrogance?

Still think you are where you were three years back?

Are you hell bent on making me cry whilst I write this?

No, son, we just need you to understand how important this work and everything you're doing is. How easy would it have been to stay with the ex-girlfriend?

Really easy. She was everything any man could have asked for.

Yes she was and still is, but why was she not for you?

Soon as she moved in, I had this feeling she would have been my second divorce if we got married.

Did you see it as fear?

Nope, more like a premonition.

Did you make the "right" choice?

Damn right I did.

So why feel guilt over the way it finished?

Because it's what I do. Get girls to fall in love with me and then fuck up their lives.

Firstly, you can't make someone fall in love with you, that's the reason we have free will. Secondly, marrying her would have been more painful for both of you.

So as I was told by my mom, I just have to accept that I am a twat.

Just stop. Even if no one takes anything from our teachings, can you please take one thing: if we do not label our creations, why does humankind?

Because, a frog is a fucking frog. It's not like it's going to become a prince after you fuck it.

Those are not the labels we are talking about. What label was placed on you by your mom?

Which mother are we talking about, my real mother or biological one?

Let's discuss both.

I'm being dramatic. My real mother (biological) does love me unconditionally.

I'll stop you there son: does any of humankind love unconditionally?

I fucking hope so.

What do you call unconditional love?

When you have the other person's best interest at heart; where you love them with every bit of you.

Please son, stop lying.

Lol, I actually don't fucking know, I was going to google it.

So let's take the first part, the other person's best interest at heart. What you think that might be is different to what other people might think it is, as you are basing it on a judgement and opinion.

Don't most people want the same things in life? Sex, drugs and rock and roll, baby.

Please stop trying to be funny. You have a 20-year-old friend who you love unconditionally, and he has never had sexual interaction with anyone - what would you think the best thing is for him?

Well lol, I would get him a shag, as 20 years old is two years too old.

What would a friend who is religious say for him to do?

To go touch young kids lol?

Really, son? Is that all you can say?

Come on that was a little funny. He would say stay celibate till you get married.

So both of you have opinions on what would be best for him, but at any point have any of you two asked what he wants?

So all mighty what does he want?

Truth be told, if you asked him what he thinks he wants and what he actually wants, they would be two different things.

So humankind knows fuck all about unconditional love. Is that what you're trying to say?

When have you felt unconditional love?

When I connect to the source, god, spirit, angels, whatever word you want to use.

So does your biological mom love you unconditionally, or are there conditions?

There are conditions.

Would you say your ex-girlfriend fell within the parameters of those conditions?

Yes she did.

Would you like to write what these conditions are or were?

She had to brown (Indian), Sikh, decent-looking, professional and a nice person.

Out of those five things which mattered to you?

Being a nice person.

So you wanted to spend your life with someone who was only 20% of what you wanted?

It just feels like you are justifying my shit behaviour.

Chapter one my son: there is no right or wrong behaviour.

But that doesn't work in the real world.

Okay, let's talk about your spiritual mom: would you say she has ever been judgemental?

No, I would say she has not, but what has that got to do with where I am now?

So three years ago would you say you were arrogant, egotistic and judgemental, and more importantly are you that person now?

No I am not.

So where are you now?

Slightly better than the way I was three years back?

A lot better my son.

Okay I accept that my ex-girlfriend was not what I wanted, but why did it feel so right?

Because sometimes, my son, humankind's wants, desires and needs get mixed up.

Are desires and wants not the same thing?

Okay son, so let's work it out: what do you want?

I want the happy ever after.

What do you desire?

The happy ever after, being rich so I don't need to work, a body to die for, and a partner who is sexy as fuck.

What do you need?

Lol, I actually have no idea of what I need.

Son, it's okay to say.

But how do I say it, when it just brings up shit?

What is it you truly need?

I just want to feel safe.

Why is it so hard to admit?

Because than I just sound like the whole "poor me, spent so much time working on it, it can't keep coming back to my childhood".

Okay, son, we will come back to it. What do you think you are on earth for?

To learn lessons.

What was the lesson of the ex-girlfriend?

Don't go for someone that will make my family happy, go for someone that will make me happy.

But son, let's accept the fact that no one can make you happy.

I get that.

But do you really get it, son?

Yeah I do. To be honest I'm really happy most of the time but I do have my moments.

All of humankind has its moments, but it's okay not to be okay.

Yes I get it.

Son, what do you want from this lifetime?

I want it all.

Okay, define what you call "it all"?

Helping humankind to a higher vibration, the family, the love, I would say unconditional love but I can't get that, can I!

But son, you already get unconditional love, just not from where you expect it to come from.

I get it from you.

Yes you do son, the same as humankind does, but not everyone feels it. The family part, you are already here, the love has never stopped, and the helping humankind part, you have done more in the last two years than most do in their lifetimes.

But it still feels like there is so much more to do.

What is the rush?

Truth be told there is no rush, but I want to look back at my life and be proud of what I have achieved.

What is it you want to achieve?

I want to help humankind get to a higher vibration, I want them to be more spiritually awake.

Son that does not answer the question. What do you want to achieve?

I get where you're going with this, but I want to achieve it.

Son, again, what is it you truly want?

Honestly I have everything I want, yeah the love life could be better but I believe the time will come when it needs to.

Is that the truth?

Nope, it's not. Sometimes I believe the person has come and gone.

How does that make you feel?

A bit sad, but deep down I know there is a bigger picture I don't understand.

Son, how about we simplify your life. It's not your responsibility to help humankind get to a higher vibration, so to speak. You have responsibility for one thing - your life - and that's it. So what is it you want?

Enhanced spiritual connection, love in its truest form, the ability to make a positive impact on the world.

Would you say your wants reflect what most of humankind wants?

I can't speak for all of humankind, but I think a lot would want true love. Not sure about the spiritual connection, but I do believe most also want to do the "right" thing and make a positive impact on the world.

My son, you do sometimes live in a dream world. Most of the humankind wants more money to buy more things they don't want.

I disagree, I think humankind has progressed.

It has, but everyone has their place.

Are we born in that place or do we become that place?

Son, when we refer to a place it's not in the sense you're thinking of.

Okay, explain.

So everyone has a place: they are exactly where they need to be.

How does that even work? Someone just gets run over, I can assure you they did not want to be there, someone is in jail, don't think they want to be there - the list goes on.

Son, we never spoke about their want to be only their need to be.

You're frustrating me.

It's okay. The simplest way to explain it is, humankind is here to learn lessons and move on.

I am fed up of my lessons. They just feel like they are dragging on.

Son, even when the lesson is the same lesson, it's never the same.

That doesn't even make sense, the same lesson is never the same lesson?

Imagine in this lifetime you have come to fall in love; that lesson would be different in each lifetime.

Fuck me.

What's wrong?

Are we here only to learn one lesson at a time?

Yes and no. Lessons learnt are as long as you need them to be - your lesson is still being learnt.

What's the point? I'm at the point where I actually don't want to play anymore. I am done.

What are you done with?

The lesson of love.

How do you know your lessons are about love?

All I want to do is love unconditionally, yet you told me there is no such thing.

Son, just because… what are you getting frustrated with?

Honestly, I just feel hopeless when it comes to my love life. I feel so stupid, used, useless, frustrated and angry, and before you say it I know there is light at the end of the tunnel, but how much more hurt and pain do I have to go through?

Like I said, son, how long your lessons last is up to you.

Also, why do you keep changing from "we" to "I"? Make your fucking mind up.

This is beyond human understanding.

Again with that bullshit, simplify it for me then.

I go from a sole entity to a joint entity as I require. It's to balance the alpha and beta energy waves.

I thought it was male and female energy you had?

Like I said, it's beyond human understanding. Let's get back on track: what do you think your lesson is?

My lesson is to fuck till I die.

Stop being such a drama queen.

Lol, I'm not sure what my lesson is, but I feel like it's a journey of love as all other aspects of my life are fantastic.

Okay, so let's go with what you think your lesson is. What have you learnt so far this lifetime?

I fall in and out of love quicker than a hooker drops her pants.

Okay, so in your head you think you have truly loved?

In my head I feel the love every night.

That's a lie, my son.

Okay, at the moment I feel like I have gone backwards.

Why do you feel like you have gone backwards?

Because I went through that stage of empty sex again.

How did it make you feel?

Honestly? It made me feel dirty.

If it makes you feel like that, why carry on?

That's my circle of abuse, so what happens is I carry on abusing myself.

Still think your lesson is about love?

Come on, you can't say my lesson in this lifetime is to deal with my child abuse.

If this is your lesson in this lifetime, would it really be that "bad"?

I honestly thought I was healed, so why would I have to carry on the lesson?

Are you honestly saying that?

No I am not.

You broke up with your ex-girlfriend in May 2017. How did you feel?

Like everything in my life was a lesson.

What was the lesson?

I am a twat?

No son, you are not a twat. What was the lesson?

I'm really struggling with this.

Let's break it down: what kind of person was she?

She was lovely, everything any man would want.

So, my son, why did you not want her?

Soon as we moved in, I know she was not for me.

So, my son, who was she for?

I did the typical British Indian thing, found a nice girl that would fit into my family.

Would she have fitted into your family?

Yeah my parents loved her.

Would you say you only went with her because it was the "right" thing to do?

Yes.

So let's expand that. You went with a girl that your mom would have approved of.

Yes and I know why now - fear of rejection.

What was your fear of rejection?

That my mom would not have accepted her.

Or was it that your mom would have rejected you? If you loved the "wrong" person.

Yes I would have been rejected as well.

Do you accept this is linked to your childhood?

I do now. I never knew how bad my fear of rejection was until recent times.

So do you think you have learnt your lesson?

No, I haven't, but I don't even know what the lesson is any more. I have forgiven my abuser, I have forgiven myself, I have learnt to love myself, what more do I need to do?

But son, is that not the beauty of the journey?

I just want to be told what to do. I am fed up of going around in circles.

It's no one's job to tell humankind how to live its life.

I get that, but how does that help me?

It gives you a purpose.

So frustrating, you're making me feel anxious.

Why do you feel anxious?

In my head I have dealt with my childhood.

We agree with you.

So why are you going back to it?

Son, just because you have dealt with the past does not mean everything is healed.

So I still have more healing to do?

Son, everyone does. Let's say you have dealt with your child abuse; have you dealt with your fear of rejection?

In my head I have, last eleven months I have worked on it.

How have you worked on it?

Chapter 13 – Fear of rejection

Wow, must be a serious topic for it to get a chapter all by itself.

So, son, how have you worked on your fear of rejection?

By asking girls way out of my league on dates, so they say no, now I know how my mates at university felt lol.

Stop being silly.

It's true, I have been rejected more in the last year than I have in my whole lifetime.

How many women actually said no to you?

When you say no, do you mean no to sex or no in general?

How many said no that you actually wanted?

Ermmmm, none.

Why is the figure at zero?

Basically had first dates with three different girls who all never wanted a second date.

How did that make you feel?

Rejected to start with but then relieved.

Why relieved?

Because deep down I knew they were not right for me.

So, son, ask the question.

Errrrmmmm, I don't fucking know, what question?

Okay I'll ask it for you: would any of them have been more than fun? No son, they would not have been more than fun.

That kind of made me sad.

Why?

Because they were the best from a bad bunch.

So I'll ask again: how have you dealt with your fear of rejection?

The hard part is, I have to accept that I don't think I have.

Then let's work on the question you keep asking: where is she? You know the answer.

Yes I do, I'm the one that's blocking my happy ever after?

Yes you are.

So, wise one, how do I sort it out?

I sense sarcasm in your tone.

Do you blame me? Just feels like I'm back where I started.

And if you were, would that be such a "bad" thing?

Yes it would be, as it's frustrating - I am no closer to completing my circle.

And to you, completing your circle would be what?

Okay, spiritually I have progressed so much, physically I'm in good shape, financially I can't complain at all, inner healing could be better but that is an ongoing project, then the love life part is an absolute shambles, but I don't struggle to meet girls, online dating has made it so much easier.

So would you say your love life and healing need work?

Yes they do.

So if I said you have to heal more before the special someone comes into your life, how would you react?

I would accept that, and heal away.

What do you think you need healing for?

Well, the title of the chapter is fear of rejection so I'm assuming that's what I need to work on.

Well son, you are assuming wrong.

Okay, so what do I need to heal from?

What have you done to help yourself heal?

I meditate every day, writing this book has helped me release the hate of the past, I've stopped having sex with people who I have no emotional attachment to.

Has it helped?

Yes and no, meditation yes, releasing the past yes, stopping the empty sex, I don't know, truth be told I only did it as I thought it might help me manifest the long-term partner.

So how has your mindset changed?

What the fuck has this got to do with fear of rejection?

Patience, my son. How has your mindset changed?

From just wanting to fuck attractive women, I now only want women who I could have a future with.

How many girls right now on your phone could you have a future with?

Quite a few.

How many do you want a future with?

None.

Why not?

Just felt like something was missing. I want it all, inner and outer beauty, fun loving, deep connection, that's what I desire.

Would you say your intent is right?

Or course it is, there is nothing I would not do for this person.

So, son, let's agree that there is nothing wrong with your love life.

How the fuck can you say that? Where is she lol?

She is already in your life, but the fear of rejection will stop you approaching her.

I take it you're referring to the girl from the gym?

Yes we are.

That just sounds so cringe. I don't even know her name, she doesn't even know my name, I don't even know if she is single and I don't even think she notices me. Most importantly I don't want to be that creepy guy, just seems really weird.

Writing a book about having a conversation with god does not sound "weird" at all?

Writing this book is so much easier than chatting up a girl that's not interested.

Who told you she was not interested?

No one, but as a guy you just know when someone is not interested.

Son, let's get back to your list of what you want in a relationship. Inner and outer beauty, fun loving, deep, meaningful connection and love beyond human understanding.

Yes that pretty much sums it up.

How much emphasis would you put on the outer beauty?

Honestly about 10%.

So let's say she wants the same things but has an emphasis on outer beauty at about 20%, does she know you enough to be interested?

No she does not.

Son, this is what you are normally used to; you meet a girl who wants you because she is attracted to your outside, and in the past that's been enough for you.

That's true.

But now you want something of substance you will not attract those kinds of girls into your life, and even if you do, you will not pay attention to them.

Part of me actually wants to be rejected by this girl in the gym.

Why do you think she will reject you?

Girls like that don't go for guys like me.

Why are you being so judgemental about yourself?

I don't even know.

Let's say you are basing it on outer beauty. Would you say you have dated girls that have been more "beautiful"?

Yes I have.

So why do you think she will say no?

As I have got older I have become more insecure about my external body.

But son, you have so much more to offer now to a partner than you ever have.

I know that I have so much to offer.

You have not become insecure about your external beauty; it's your fear of rejection that's coming through as you get older.

How do I stop that fear of rejection?

You are approaching this in an incorrect manner.

So how should I approach it?

There are two different things, healing on one side and fear of rejection on the other.

I don't get it.

They are not dependent on each other. You could be 99% healed and still have 90% fear of rejection.

I thought the more you healed the less your fear of rejection should be.

That would be the logical way of looking at it, but that's not how it works. Let's use your fear of rejection as an example.

Go for it.

How far on the healing path do you think you are?

60 to 70% I would say.

How often do you have a negative thought about someone or feel very sad?

That's a tough question, I would say once or twice a day if that.

How often do you have positive or happy thoughts of people?

All the time.

Do you remember when we said healing never stops?

Yes, why?

Your healing is directly linked to your thoughts and feelings. The more negative thoughts you have, the more negative feelings you have and the more healing you need.

Fuck me lol, I'm not as broken as I thought I was.

So, son, when was the last time you had a negative thought about someone else?

I actually can't remember, truth is I'm not that way inclined, I just leave people to it.

When was the last time you had a negative thought about yourself?

Not really negative, just thought a few weeks ago, "wow I have put some weight on, I better get training".

Do you think like that now?

Not really, the harder I train, the better I look.

When was the last time you had a negative feeling?

I get one every few days.

What is that feeling?

Being lonely, desiring company.

So why don't you change that and have company all the time?

Been there and done that, does not change that feeling, if anything makes it worse.

So, let's ignore the desire of wanting company as that doesn't get rid of the negative feeling. Let's focus on the feeling of being lonely. How does it make you feel?

I can't really describe the feeling, it's actually not that bad, if I'm honest I just shake the feeling and move on.

Okay son, let's say you are 90% healed: how does that make you feel?

I don't know, it doesn't feel like 90%, but who am I to complain lol, how do I get that last 10%?

The last 10% is ongoing. Every day you keep doing what you're doing. Let's address the feeling of loneliness.

Do we have to?

Yes, my son, as a lot of humankind has similar struggles.

Go for it.

The loneliness is directly linked to your fear of rejection.

I kind of thought that was coming. So how do I overcome it?

You need to change your approach, as you don't have to overcome it. Just be okay with fact it is there and accept it for what it is.

And what is it?

It is whatever you want it to be. It can be as small as you want or as big as you want.

I don't even know what I want it to be.

How is this making you feel?

A little confused, but I feel relief at the same time. So is the loneliness blocking the happy ever after?

No, my son, as you can change that feeling in an instant.

So I'm assuming it's the fear of rejection?

Yes it is, son.

So how do I work on it?

You're not going to like what is next.

I know I'm not, but let's hear it.

Your fear of rejection comes down to issues with your mom and childhood.

I don't want to be that person that links everything to something so long ago, it's been dealt with.

Yes, my son, your child abuse has been dealt with but your fear of rejection has not. We said childhood, not child abuse, but naturally you linked it yourself as that's what you thought it was about.

So what is it about?

Even if your child abuse did not occur, your childhood would still have left you with scars.

Nah that's bullshit, apart from the child abuse my childhood was fine, my family are really nice.

Let us stop you there son. We are not referring to your interactions with your family. Let's look at the wider audience - as a child, how did you feel growing up?

Honestly, I felt on the outside, isolated, the people I called friends I actually never understood.

Would you say you were a people pleaser?

Not at all, some people like me, some don't, I actually don't care.

What would you say the core of your fear of rejection comes from?

Being from an Indian Sikh background, from a young age you have it installed in your head you will do x, you will become y, and marry z.

Would you say you achieved those things?

Not at all, never got a degree, I'm divorced, talking to dead people, so all in all, not really the Indian thing to do.

How do you feel now?

I come to a quick conclusion, the ones that will reject me are judgemental and are not even on my level, so why should I care?

Are we talking in relationships or in general?

In general, most people spend lifetimes trying to please others because of fear of rejection, I'll always do what I want to do.

So why do you fear rejection when it comes to your love life?

I don't even know, I don't want to be that sleazy pervert that hits on women.

So then don't be.

Well that's why I struggle to even converse sometimes.

Why are you lying, my son? You do not struggle to converse, but the fear of rejection from a person you don't even know grips you, though it actually does not matter.

Logically I know it doesn't matter but why am I struggling then?

Would you say you lack confidence?

Why does it feel like we are going around in circles?

That's because we are.

How do I break it?

By acknowledging how you feel and working through it.

I have a fear of rejection, now please sort it out.

Son, please stop.

It's frustrating being here, it really is. I know where I want to be, I know where I will be, but right now, fuck no.

How about learning to enjoy the journey?

The journey? Never been one to play the victim, but don't you think I have had enough pain for one lifetime?

Finally some progress.

How the fuck is that progress? You're just pissing me off.

Because, my son...

No, don't "my son" me bullshit, simple, how do I deal with the fear of rejection?

Firstly you need to understand that fear of rejection takes different forms.

What do you mean?

So let's take your fear of rejection over the last four years, from the fear of being rejected by your mother to the fear of being rejected by society.

I don't give a fuck what society thinks.

If that was true, why you do struggle to speak to the girl in the gym?

I don't want to be that guy.

Then don't be that guy. All the women you have been with and now you come to a point where a boy can't speak to a girl?

I can't stop laughing, you're actually right, since when did I become so scared of rejection?

Humankind goes through lifetimes being scared of rejection. Do you even know what you are scared of?

I thought it would be her saying no, but more of coming across as a pervert or inappropriate.

That's not what you are scared of. You are scared of what people would think if they found out you tried to chat this girl up.

It's true, I just don't want to look like a dickhead.

Welcome to humankind's true struggle: they are so concerned with what others think, they neglect what they want.

How do I stop being that person?

At the moment you are waiting at the door, and it is fully open. All you have to do is walk through it.

Sounds so simple, yeahhhhhh.

In your case, right now all you have to do is talk to the girl and ask her out. In other people's cases it could be finally doing what they really want to do: contacting a lost friend, saying sorry, the list goes on.

So let me get this right. For me to walk through that door all I have to do is ask this girl out?

For you, yes, my son.

I feel scared and I don't know why.

Do you think you're the first or last person that will ask her out?

No I am not.

What's the worst that can happen?

Says no and laughs at me.

Let's bring it all up to the surface: what else can happen?

Laughs at me, calls me names just like people did when I was younger because I was fat.

So your fear of rejection is linked to your body?

Yes it is, even though I am in really good shape, but the past still gives me pain.

So child abuse aside, what was your childhood like?

I'm struggling as I can't complain, my childhood did have good moments, and my parents did the best they could. And I accept it could have been a lot worse.

Son, this is not the moment to show gratitude. How difficult was your childhood?

I can't remember a birthday I did not cry, so due to the child abuse I ate a lot and was overweight, had man boobs and was regularly made fun of.

Do people make fun of your body now?

No, I can't remember the last time someone made fun of my body.

So why do you still carry the pain in your heart?

I don't know.

So when are you going to start talking to the girl from the gym?

In a few weeks once I have a six pack.

If she is the kind of girl that would only want you if you had a six pack what would you say?

She doesn't deserve a person like me in her life.

How much of humankind do you think can relate to that? Always trying to be smarter, prettier, richer, more fashionable, more popular just to attract, maintain and sustain "love"?

A lot.

But, my son, they don't have to, you don't have to. That fear of rejection has no power over you. How does that make you feel?

I feel stupid but relieved.

Do you not see the light you have to offer? You spend all this time helping others; you see their light but neglect your own.

This book is not about me.

This book and your life are not about you, but you're the one living the pain of it. Don't you think it's time you gave yourself a break?

I can't give myself a break, as I have so much to give.

We understand you have so much to give, but at what price?

I don't even know the price, but what else do I have to do apart from giving? No matter how hard things have been it could be worse, I'm just grateful.

How hard things were, or how hard things are?

A bit of both.

Is it not time to learn to manage expectations?

Chapter 14 – Managing the self

You know I can't manage myself?

Why do you say that?

Because I have no idea how to do it.

Do you even know what it involves?

Yeah, of course I do, typical time management bullshit.

No, my son, managing the self does not focus on things that are not relevant.

What do you mean?

What is the most important thing to you?

Right now, I would say Friday and Saturday night lol.

No son, what do you really care about?

My niece and two nephews.

Would you say the love you have for them is time relevant?

Of course not, whether I spend two hours or five minutes I still love them.

So your love for them is not time relevant.

Okay, I agree with that, but what does that have to do with managing the self?

To truly manage yourself, you need to understand the core of your desires.

That's so easy, sleep, eat and have sex.

You have done that for the last 20 years of your life. Do you feel you're any closer to being self-managed?

Nope.

So let's understand your true core desires: love, giving and direction.

They are so open and generic, what does any of this have to do with managing expectations or yourself?

Your desires are very closely linked to your expectations, which in turn affect your ability to manage yourself.

Are we referring to self-expectations or expectations of others?

Both.

Managing my own expectations is not that difficult, but I struggle to manage other people's expectations.

So my son, let's simplify it for you: what do you desire?

I desire what most want, love, health, wealth and direction, I would assume a lot of people want the same things.

Out of the things you mentioned above, how many would you say you desire, and how many of them do you want because you have been conditioned to want them?

I would struggle to answer that question as I am not sure.

Okay. If you could only do one thing this lifetime what would you do?

I would help others.

How would you like to help others?

By showing them a better way to live.

If that is all you want, then you have already achieved that through this book.

Yeah, but there is so much more to do.

Who told you that you have so much more to do?

I tell myself I have so much more to do.

Could this be classified as self-expectation?

Call it whatever you want, I just know I have so much to do and so much to give.

Where does it finish?

What do you mean?

When does the giving finish?

Hopefully never, I hope I spend all this lifetime giving as much as I can.

How many people do you want to help? One million? Two million?

As many as I can.

Let's say you have a choice between the happy ever after and helping ten people. Which one do you want?

That's a stupid question, I know I can have both.

Just a question my son, just answer it.

I would help the ten people.

Okay, how about helping one person or the happy ever after?

One person over the happy ending all day long.

So why don't we focus on that one person now? And start helping yourself?

Sounds so cliché, "let me help myself".

Why do you struggle to put yourself first?

Because there are so many more people in the world that need the love, help, whatever you want to call it more than I do.

But you're not responsible for them; you are only responsible for you.

I know that! You fucking remind me constantly. But I can't accept that, I will not change the life I have, which is the life of giving.

What would you really like to give?

The ability for humankind to feel pure love.

What if that affects their free will?

Who would not want to feel true love?

You.

That's a bit mean, actually that's a really twat comment to make.

You run away, every time it comes to giving yourself true love.

Are you referring to my inability to commit?

No son, you do not have commitment issues.

It does feel like I do, sometimes.

Let's address it.

Just feels like I want things I can't have, and when I get them I don't want them.

You have gone from lesson to lesson when it comes to your relationships.

I accept that, but how many more girls am I going to hurt? I don't want to hurt any more.

Then don't hurt them. The next person you date, commit to them for a lifetime.

But that would not be fair on them or me.

Why would it not be fair?

Because I believe they should be loved purely, and if I can't give that to them why should I hold them back?

So would you say you sacrifice your own happiness for others?

Hell no, I have always been the one walking away or breaking up from all my long-term relationships. So I'm not the victim or "poor me" kind of guy.

Let's go back to a question we asked you earlier: happy ever after or helping one person?

You know the answer, helping one person.

Let's leave that there. If you don't understand the question then it's not time.

You fucking what? Just spit it out all ready.

You still feel some kind of guilt over your past relationships.

I'm not a robot, of course I do, why would I not?

Have they moved on?

We have already had this conversation, of course they have.

So why don't you?

I'm fucking trying, I just seem to fuck it up a lot lol.

Let's talk about your last three dates.

What does any of this have to do with managing yourself or expectations?

You will see in time, my son.

Well where do I even start?

Let's say the last two dates and the gym girl.

Hmmm, they might read this one day lol.

Trust me son, you are safe.

Date number one went well, met up, got on, but I think I was too pushy.

In what way do you think you were pushy?

Well, I actually came to a conclusion that I actually don't know how to date.

Explain, my son.

Okay, from the start, went on a first date, went well, supposed to organise a second one, she said when are you free? I was brutally honest, I said all the time apart from Sunday mornings (take my nephew football) and Monday evenings (meditation class).

Then what happened?

She asked which day I would suggest, I said, Thursday, Friday, Saturday, Tuesday or Wednesday lol.

Why is that pushy?

We had seen each other on the Wednesday, so apparently you're not supposed to see someone more than once a week when you first meet them.

Would you say you are a needy person?

Hell no, I do not rely on any one, I have my own stuff on.

So why do you think you are pushy?

Maybe pushy's not the right word to use, overbearing is better.

Why would you call yourself overbearing?

Well I actually worked it out a few days back, so this is what I got advised, if someone texts you, you're supposed to wait a few hours before you text back.

How did that make you feel?

Unnatural, for example, if one of my mates messaged me, work messaged me, even if my football team messaged me, I would message back soon as I could.

We know you are getting frustrated, my son, as you are trying to see the relevance, but I promise you it will come through. Let's talk about the second person.

Met on a night out, added me on Facebook, wanted to know more about this book and the first two versions, so I sent her a free copy.

Then what happened?

She read the first 11 chapters then went on to say she did not want to date a guy that was broken.

How did that make you feel?

I kind of got it, as I have done that in the past, I don't mind healing the world but just not at home as well.

What actually hurt you?

Truth is, even if I can't prove it, humankind has a saying, the abused become the abusers.

Would you ever do that?

I don't even need to answer that question, in my head if someone can't see the impact it had on my life, who in their right mind would do that to someone else?

So we take that as a no?

Take that as a fuck no!

How much did it hurt?

A lot.

Why did it hurt?

I am done with showing people my value, truth is if they can't see it then they don't deserve me in their lives.

A lot of humankind makes that statement.

I know they do, but I will never change my statement. I now know my value, not my fault if they can't see it.

Welcome to stage one of managing the self: knowing your own value.

Come on, got to be more to it than that.

Why does there have to be more?

That seems way too simple.

Why does humankind have to make everything more complex? We want life to be easy and

simple; once you learn your value you can start managing the self.

Okay, what next?

What happened with the gym girl?

Nothing much, we started talking, I sent her a copy of this book and she became funny with me.

How did she become funny?

Honestly, she's carrying way too much baggage from the past, something I said triggered that, all I saw was a person that needs a lot of love and healing.

So what did you decide to do?

Nothing at all, I am done with healing at home, I did that with past partners.

Welcome to stage two: actually learning the lessons of the past. How many weeks did it take you?

About six weeks.

How long did it take you in the past?

Two years, so what's stage three?

There are only two stages, my son.

What the fuck do you mean? Got to be more.

Why does there have to be more, my son?

So all I have to do is, know my own value, learn the lessons of the past and I'm onto a winner of knowing how to manage myself?

Yes.

Okay, so how does that help with managing expectations?

Simple. You know your own value: you know what you do and don't want.

That doesn't even make sense, can you please dumb it down for me?

What is your value?

How long is a piece of string? How can my value relate to all of humankind?

Forgot about humankind. What is your self-value?

I am loving, caring and giving.

When you were with your ex, what were the expectations on you?

To get married.

So why did you not?

Because it did not feel loving or caring. I'm really confused now, you're not making sense.

Okay, my son, through your life you have been given expectations, which have influenced the way you are. Today we worked out the core of what you want. Now you can stop looking at other people's expectations and focus on what you want.

Managing the self is all about working out what you want?

It's the basic step. Once you know your own value you will work towards doing and thinking in ways that enhance and agree with your own value.

Okay, that makes sense, so I need to work out my self-value and work towards it?

You don't have to work towards it, as your self-value is what you think of yourself.

I get that but you need to be more practical.

If you think you deserve to be treated poorly, people will and you will accept it. As soon as you

know your own value you can stop that from happening and only do what you want to do.

Okay, what have the lessons got to do with it?

The lessons help you work out what you actually want.

Then what? A unicorn appears?

No, son. Once you know what you want, you stop working towards other people's expectations.

Explain please?

Okay, let's use your example: you want to love, give and be happy?

Yes.

So you do what you think will help you feel like that, and if something does not, you change it.

You know what's coming don't you, if someone is not happy in their marriage, should they just walk?

Yes they should walk, as the reasons behind why they are staying together are what?

Other people's expectations. But that is easier said than done.

No, my son. Once someone knows what they want their lives will be so much better.

Chapter 15- The choice we all have

What choice do you think we are referring to?

The choice to be happy or not.

Why do you think it's to do with that?

Simple, I have read enough books that suggest in life we have two choices in any situation, to be happy about it or not.

Do you think that is the most important choice in life?

To me it is, as I see too many people being sad, all they have to do is change the way they react to things.

We agree with that to a certain extent but there are more important choices to make in life.

Like what?

Humans have three main choices in life: to live in the past, present or future.

Okay I understand parts of that, the past is normally related to pain, future is normally related to hope, and the present is normally forgotten.

Which one do you think is most important?

To me it's the future, as it motivates me to be more and do more every day.

Is that the only reason you think it's most important?

Well, the other two are lesser in my eyes, the past reminds me of the pain I have been through, the present is nice but I know the future is better.

What makes you so adamant that the future is so good?

Hope, allows me to believe that there is so much to give.

As a rough guess how much of your life was spent thinking of the past, present and future?

60% of the past, 30% future, 10% present, but then through forgiveness it changed.

What did it change to?

15% past, 70% future and 15% present.

Do you think this is a "good" balance?

What happened to "there is no good or bad"?

We are not the ones judging you, you are.

I know my balance is better than it was in the past, but I need to live in the present.

Why do you say you need to live in the present?

Because I have been told I am letting life pass me by as I am so focused on where I want to be and the future.

What do you want?

I want that life I see, but I want it now.

Would you say you deserve that life?

You're being a bit judgemental today.

Again, son, this is not about us, it's about you.

Give me a few minutes to think about it... Of course I deserve it.

Why did it take you a few minutes? It was a simple question.

Because I was weighing up, seeing if I have done enough good in my life.

Do you not see how judgemental you are being on yourself?

Yes I do, what can I say, I am still a work in progress.

What are you working on and trying to progress to?

Everything, I can't stop wanting more.

Okay, why do you want more?

More money, better health and better relationships.

No son, I'm not asking what areas you want more in but why do you want more?

I actually don't even know why I want more, also it depends on what area you're referring to.

Why do you want more money?

Easy answer, I want an easier life.

How would more money give you an easier life?

More money means I can spend more time doing the things I love and less time doing the things I don't love.

How much money do you need in essence to survive?

In essence a lot less than what I need now.

How much money do you need to maintain the lifestyle you have?

Around £1600.00 a month.

How much a month are you making now?

More than that.

So why not reduce your working hours and make less?

Because one day I hope to have a family, families are not cheap!

So you want to make more money for an event that has not happened?

It's called planning, you Muppet.

So would you call planning living in the present?

No it's not, it's living in the future, but it is an essential part of living.

Why is it an essential part of living?

Worst part is I don't even plan that much, just trying to save some money so I can have more time to spend with my loved ones at a later stage of life.

Why are you getting frustrated?

I don't even know.

Can we reflect on the last few weeks?

What for!

The question that keeps popping up in your life: are you okay?

I don't even know, it's a real strange place to be as I don't know the answer to that question.

What do you feel?

That's the thing, I am struggling to feel, just feel really numb and distant. Kind of feels like dying.

Would that be such a bad thing, to die right now?

I know this is going to sound fucked up, but I'm kind of excited to die.

Why are you excited, my son?

Hopefully it's better than being here.

Is here such a bad place to be?

Sometimes yes and sometimes no, am I depressed?

No my son, not at all, just at the next stage of enlightenment.

Wtf is that? Not giving a shit?

You are becoming emotionless, which is kind of detachment at its peak.

So what happens next?

What would you like to happen next?

To rain gold bricks and become rich.

Okay, we will play the game. You're now rich, what do you want more of now?

Fuck yeah, I can now go travel the world and party.

You can do that now.

Yes that's true, kind of killed the fun of it.

Do you even enjoy travelling?

Honestly, no I don't, I enjoy being at home and around my loved ones.

So why did you travel last year?

Thought it might make me happy.

Did it?

Not at all.

So with all that money, what do you want to do with it?

Save it for the family to come.

So you're living in the future with that one. Why do you want better health?

I love playing football, as I have got older I have had to train harder to maintain what I have.

What's your fear?

That I get that bad I have to stop playing.

Is that the case now?

No, I am doing okay.

So you want better health for an event that has not happened yet? What do we call that?

Living in the future.

Next one: why do you want better relationships?

Everyone wants better relationships.

We are not talking about everyone, we are talking about you. Which relationships could be better?

To be honest all my relationships are really good apart from the one with my mom.

So how would you improve your relationship with your mom?

I have accepted it for what it is, and accepted it will never get better.

So why do you want to improve it?

It would make my life easier.

How would it make your life easier?

The relationship has started to affect other members of the family, which I think is unfair.

So why don't you change the relationship with your mother?

I have tried, but it's never going to happen.

So accept it's not in your control.

Easier said than done.

No, my son, once you accept it, you understand that you cannot change the outcome.

If I can't change the outcome what happened to free will?

The outcome is not your lesson, it is your mother's. So which other relationships would you like to change?

Well if I can't change the outcome, then none.

So would you say wanting better relationships was living in the present?

Up till about five minutes back I would have said it was about improving the future, now it's about the present.

So, my son, what aspects do you want more in?

You have covered them all.

I'll ask that question again: what aspects do you want more in?

Nah, I'm not going to be that guy.

Son, wanting to improve your love life, or wanting more in your love life, is not a "bad" thing.

I know that but it can't keep coming down to that. One hand you tell me not to live in the future i.e. plan for kids and then you're saying it's okay to want more in your love life.

What do you want?

Change the world.

Again you're looking into the future.

Does it have to be in the present?

Yes it does.

Why does it? Why can't it be in the future?

Because my son, humankind needs to learn to live in the present.

I'm trying to, but without hope what's the point?

How much of what you want is what you want, and not what others expect of you?

Honestly, all I want is pure love.

Son you already have that. Once you start living in the present, you will see love all around you. Just slow down, time is not important, focus on what you really want. Love.

Easier said than done.

Every time you meet someone you are already six months down the line in your head. Just one hour after meeting someone you think you know where it is going. You filter them into three categories: short, medium and long term.

Talk about being fucking judgemental.

No, my son, we are not judging what you are doing. Let's change those categories to what they really are: past, present and future.

I have never actually looked at it like that.

"Short term" is what you call it, but a lot of these girls remind you of what?

Girls from my past, so they just end up being fun.

So, my son, could we conclude that short term flings are fun and you're living in the past?

Yeah maybe, but I'm not 100% convinced.

Why do you have short term fun with these girls?

Most of the time it's a sexual release.

Why do you want a sexual release?

Because it feels good.

How do you know it feels good?

Fuck my life, if it did not feel good why would I do it?

How do you know it feels good?

Because a few weeks back I felt it. It's something called having a memory.

So what we can say is, you are trying to replicate a feeling from your past?

Okay, I get it, yeah you could say a sexual release is linked to your past.

Why do you put girls into a long term category?

Going to sound so Judas lol, I make a judgement based on what I see and feel, from that I work out if they could potentially be a long term partner.

So you're basing it on what someone says and shows you?

Yes and no, just being around someone you can tell.

Would you say this is living in the future?

100% it is, as in your mind you are busy playing the "what could happen" game or "what you want to happen" game.

How many girls have been in these two categories?

Most have fallen in both.

No my son, all have fallen into those two categories.

Yeah you're right, they have.

How many girls you been with for a medium term, i.e. living in the present with?

None.

Welcome to the next stage of enlightenment.

What’s that?

Chapter 16 – How to find true love

Why are you putting off writing this chapter, my son?

I feel like a fraud, how can I write this whilst being single? should I not be already half way there?

How do you know you're not half way there?

I don't even have one person in my life that I can call a potential.

What would you call potential?

I already know where this is going, a potential is living in the future not in the present.

Yes you are right son. So how many girls have you met that have been short or long term?

All of them.

Is there any girl that you have regrets over? That is, you would change the outcome of your relationship with?

One sticks out, but looking at it, it's not regret over what we had, but what we could have had.

Living in the future?

Yeah, don't get me wrong, really nice, we got on, but I was going through my arsehole stage.

Do you think she is the one that got away?

Well she has not really got away, we are still in contact due to work.

How does it make you feel when you speak to her?

Even before anything happened between us, I always liked her as she was a really nice person.

So how do you feel when you speak to her now?

I feel happy, a bit sad sometimes, but moments of excitement as well.

Why sad?

Because I treated her like a twat, so in reflection not a nice thing to do.

Why excited?

Because I know one day someone else will come into my life and have the same effect but this time I will not fuck it up.

So we could say, you feel happy in the present, sad about the past and excited about the future?

Yeah that would be a good assessment.

So do you think she is the one that got away?

Again, she has not really got away.

So why don't you be with her?

Because she is getting married, and in this world there are some things you just don't do.

Have you told her how you feel?

Yes I did.

What was the outcome?

She chose him.

How did that make you feel?

Honestly, sad for what we could have had, but then just picked myself up and went on holiday.

And what did you do on holiday?

What most sad, heartbroken men would do, hook up with someone else.

Why don't you "fight for her"?

Why should I?

Why should you not?

Because I know my own value now, if she can't see my value then she doesn't deserve to be with a person like me.

Have you allowed her to see your value?

Hmmmmm, probably not.

How many people do you allow to see your true value?

Not many.

Why not?

Most have a picture in their heads of what they think I am, so I let it be.

Is that the complete truth?

Nope, most have a picture of me that I help paint, so if or when I hurt them I feel less guilty as I come with a warning label.

What are your warning labels?

Here today, gone tomorrow, fuck everything that walks, commitment issues, pretty much sums it up.

Do you really think that is what you are? Let's work on those. Here today, gone tomorrow, what's your longest relationship?

Eight years and a marriage.

What is your shortest?

One year.

So, my son, that statement is not true. Next statement: "fuck everything that walks". You have said "no" more than you have said "yes", correct?

That's true.

We do agree you have commitment issues, but not in the context you're thinking.

Whohooooo one out of three, not bad at all lol, go on, explain.

The only commitment issue you have is you yourself. You don't allow anyone to see the true you, as you hide behind this alpha male persona, which we both know you don't have to be.

But life is so much easier when people have low or no expectations of you.

That is true, but there is a difference between having no expectations of you and you painting an untrue picture of yourself. How many see the real you?

My adopted mom and adopted sister.

And what do they see?

They see me, they care and love me for the way I am, not what I choose to show.

How many people have seen this side to you? Apart from your mom and sister.

Everyone I have had a long-term relationship with.

So the ones you thought you had a future with.

Yes.

So why don't you show everyone the true you?

Why waste my time?

Son, it takes more energy and time to pretend to be something you are not. What are you scared of?

This is going to sound silly, I'm scared of opening up to the wrong person and getting hurt.

But my son, you're hurting every time you sleep with a girl you don't love. I know this is hard for you, as all you want is boy meets girl and falls in love and has the happy ever after, but can you really say you have learnt from your past "mistakes"?

No I have not.

So what "mistakes" do you think you need to learn from?

I need to live in the present, show everyone who I really am, stop going with girls I want to save and heal.

So why not show that girl that you think got away your true self?

Because it's too late.

How do you know it's too late?

Because she is getting married.

And?

You're supposed to be the higher power and instil morals etc. into me, not encourage me to be immoral, I don't need much convincing.

We do not judge, my son. What would happen if you did tell her how you felt?

Makes things really awkward as we have a working relationship, she thinks what the fuck, or even worse she says yes.

You're lying. Work would not get awkward, what she thinks is not your choice as you have no control over it, and the truth is, if she says yes it scares you. Do you even know why?

I have no idea, because I am scared of true love?

No, son, it scares you as deep down you know she still loves you. How does that make you feel?

A bit sad.

Why?

Because I just want her to be happy.

Why do you want her to be happy?

I want everyone to be happy, that's the kind of guy I am.

So why don't you show that?

I don't know.

Why do you struggle to show who you are?

Scared of being judged, as when they judge what I am showing them it's okay as it's not me.

So who do you want to be?

I am already everything I want to be.

Is it not time to show the world who you are?

That sounds so dramatic.

It's not supposed to be dramatic, just the brutal truth. You thought finding love was this magical formula.

I actually did, I was waiting for this divine answer that was going to change my world and everyone else's.

No, my son, all you have to do is be you. Let the world see the true you. Not the mask you hide behind.

Kind of feel disappointed, seems a bit like an anti-climax, can I get my money back?

Do you know why you feel that way?

No I don't.

Because now you have the answer to everything you want.

Okay, what if one of the readers is a twat, how would they find true love?

By being themselves.

So even if a person is a twat they can find true love?

Firstly, we do not judge. True love exists for all, but they have to choose to be true to themselves.

Okay, still struggling here.

Has anyone who has seen the true you in a relationship not wanted to be with you?

They have always wanted to be with me, but deep down I know there was something missing.

What is normally missing?

The element of true love, that divine god feeling.

Have you ever felt it?

I don't think I have.

What about the girl who is getting married, would you say you loved her?

I am not sure.

Okay, we will help clarify it. She is getting married: how does that make you feel?

I am happy for her, as she deserves to be happy.

If you truly loved her, you would not be "happy for her". You would know deep down you're the only one that can truly make her happy.

That kind of sounds dark and stalkerish. No love and light there lol.

No, my son, just the truth. We hear humankind so frequently say, "I love this person and I want what's best for them." If it's true love, you are the best for them.

Fuck me, stalkerish across the world going to be charring at that, but where do you draw the line?

What do you mean by "line"?

Okay, practical world, reading that stalker shit a few lines before would say it's okay to keep chasing, what if they are chasing the wrong person?

You mean in the same way you have chosen the wrong people for the last three years based on a future that has not happened?

A but fucking harsh, and one year not three, and I don't call a 30-minute conversation chasing someone.

Welcome.

Welcome to fucking what?

The next stage of enlightenment.

Just spit it out, will you.

You now are free of the past. You have come to the conclusion yourself that it was never true love.

Don’t really feel enlightened.

How do you feel?

Kind of scared.

Do you know why you are scared?

Of the unknown?

How about we change that to excited for the unknown.

Excited, scared, it’s the same thing.

So let’s change it even further: excited to live in the present.

I kind of like that.

So, my son, you do know this is the end of the book?

Really, we done?

This book is done, yes, my son.

Nah, thought that last time and bang, two years later dragged back here.

Before we finish, do you have any questions?

Am I going to win the lottery?

Yes you are.

Fuck yeah, time to retire.

We never said how much.

Fuck nooooooo. Okay, on a serious note, why do people think every time something happens its god's doing?

That's humans going from one extreme to another, from believing there is no greater power to thinking that everything is god's will. But I hope you have discovered your reality is a manifestation of your thinking.

Does everyone find true love?

No they don't.

Is it such a bad thing if I don't?

No it's not, my son, but now that you're living in the present it's one of the most joyous emotions you can find.

I question a lot whether I am on the right path.

There is no right or wrong path, my son. Humankind has free will, but you have to

understand any path you are on is the path you choose to walk.

Will humankind ever get out of this hole?

Give or take a few billion years. You are struggling to ask more questions.

I am, as I am trying to think from the reader's point of view. Will I write more books? And if yes, what will the subject be?

Do you want to write more books, and if yes, about what?

Point made. #freewill

Closing note

I hope you have enjoyed the journey. A few people have asked why I wrote this book, and it's simple: to change the world for the better.

Now go and empower yourself with forgiveness and live the life you deserve.

Keep the journey going and stay in touch using Facebook, Twitter or Instagram, or email directly at info@ thesecretsofforgiveness.com.

Made in the USA
Lexington, KY
02 June 2019